How to Solve Word Problems in Calculus

A Solved Problem Approach

Other books in the *How to Solve Word Problems* series:

How to Solve Word Problems in Calculus

A Solved Problem Approach

Eugene Don, Ph.D.
Department of Mathematics
Queens College, CUNY

Benay Don, M.S.
Department of Mathematics
Suffolk County Community College

McGraw-Hill

New York   Chicago   San Francisco   Lisbon   London
Madrid   Mexico City   Milan   New Delhi
San Juan   Seoul   Singapore
Sydney   Toronto

Library of Congress Cataloging-in-Publication Data

Don, Eugene.
    How to solve word problems in calculus : a solved problem approach / Eugene Don,
Benay Don.
        p. cm.
    ISBN 0-07-135897-8 (pbk. : acid-free paper)
    1. Calculus—Problems, exercises, etc.   2. Word problems (Mathematics)   I. Don, Benay.
    II. Title.

    QA301 .D66   2001
    515′.076—dc21   2001030861

McGraw-Hill

A Division of The McGraw·Hill Companies

1 2 3 4 5 6 7 8 9 10   DOC/DOC   0 9 8 7 6 5 4 3 2 1

ISBN 0-07-135897-8

*The sponsoring editor for this book was Barbara Gilson, the editing supervisor was
Maureen B. Walker, and the production supervisor was Tina Cameron. It was set in
Stone Serif by TechBooks.*

Printed and bound by R. R. Donnelley & Sons Company.

McGraw-Hill books are available at special quantity discounts to use as premiums
and sales promotions, or for use in corporate training programs. For more
information, please write to the Director of Special Sales, Professional Publishing,
McGraw-Hill, Two Penn Plaza, New York, NY 10121-2298. Or contact your
local bookstore.

 This book is printed on recycled, acid-free paper containing
a minimum of 50% recycled, de-inked fiber.

Dedicated to our past and future:
Jack, Leo, Alexis, and Ariel

Contents

Preface

This book is designed to enable students of calculus to develop their skills in solving word problems. Most calculus textbooks present this topic in a cursory manner, forcing the student to struggle with the techniques of setting up and solving complex verbal problems. This book, which may be used as a supplement to all calculus textbooks, is presented in a manner that has proved so successful with the other books in the *How to Solve Word Problems* series:

- Concise definitions and discussion of appropriate theory in easily understood terms.
- Fully worked out solutions to illustrative examples.
- Supplementary problems with complete solutions.

The purpose of this book is to increase the student's confidence in his or her ability to solve word problems. The material is presented in an easy-to-understand, readable manner and if the reader is willing to invest a little time and effort, he or she will be rewarded with a skill which will prove invaluable.

Eugene Don
Benay Don

Strategies for Solving Word Problems

The power of calculus lies in its ability to solve applied problems in such diverse areas as physics, chemistry, biology, business, economics, and the social sciences. Invariably, human beings, using *words* that attempt to describe some realistic situation, pose such problems. This book addresses the difficulties many students have solving word problems in their calculus courses.

The first task in solving a word problem is to develop a *model* for the problem at hand. A mathematical model is a description of the problem in terms of variables, functions, equations, and other mathematical entities. Once it has been modeled, the second task is to solve the problem using the appropriate mathematical tools.

Setting up and solving a calculus problem from a verbal description is a skill, which is best learned by example, following appropriate guidelines. By studying the steps set forth in each chapter, you will develop techniques that can be applied to a variety of different applications.

Try to avoid memorizing procedures applicable only to specific problems. Although this will give you instant gratification when you get the correct answer, you will find that if a problem deviates even *slightly* from the one you memorized, you will be hopelessly lost. A better approach is to learn *general* procedures, which can be applied to all problems within a specific category.

Reading a word problem is not like reading a novel. Every word is important and must be clearly understood if you are to successfully arrive at the solution. Feel free to use a dictionary, if necessary, to clarify the meaning of seemingly vague words. Use your math book to clarify the meaning of any technical words used in the problem. Read and re-read the problem until it is absolutely clear what you are given and what it is you are looking for. Then, and only then, should you begin the solution.

This book contains many worked out examples. However, you must understand that there is a big difference between viewing the solution of a problem and solving the problem by yourself. When you read an example in this book, you may be able to follow every step but you should not be misled into thinking that you completely understand the solution. Learning to solve problems is like learning to play a musical instrument. You may think a musical selection is simple while watching your teacher play it with ease, but it is not until you attempt the piece yourself that you begin to see what technical difficulties actually lie within the music.

One suggestion, which you might find useful, is to pick a problem from this book and read the solution. When you think you understand what you have read, cover the solution and attempt the problem yourself. Most likely you will find that you have some difficulty. If you have trouble sneak a peek at the solution to determine the step that caused you difficulty. Then cover the solution again and continue. Repeat this process every time you get stuck.

When you finally get to the end, take a deep breath and then attempt the problem again from the beginning. You have truly mastered the problem only if you can go from the beginning to the end by yourself *without* looking at the authors' solution.

Solving word problems is more of an art than a science. Like all artistic endeavors, perfection takes practice, patience, and perseverance. You may be frustrated at first but if you follow the guidelines described in this book, you will master this all-important skill.

Chapter I

Extracting Functions from Word Problems

Calculus is the study of the behavior of *functions*. The ability to solve "real life" problems using calculus hinges upon the ability to extract a function from a given description or physical situation.

Students usually find that a word problem is easily solved once the underlying mathematical function is determined. In this chapter we discuss techniques that will form the basis for solving a variety of word problems encountered in calculus courses.

One definition of a function found in calculus texts reads:

A *function* is a rule that assigns to each number $x \, \varepsilon \, A$, a unique number $y \, \varepsilon \, B$.

In calculus, A and B are sets of real numbers. A is called the *domain* and B the *range*. It is important to understand that a function is not a number, but a *correspondence* between two sets of numbers. In a practical sense, one may think of a function as a relationship between y and x. The important thing is that there be *one, and only one*, value of y corresponding to a given value of x.

EXAMPLE I

If $y = x^2 + 5x + 2$, then y is a function of x. For each value of x there is clearly one and only one value of y. However, if the

I

equation $x^2 + y^2 = 25$ defines the correspondence between x and y, then y is *not* a function of x. If $x = 3$, for example, then y could be 4 or -4.

Functions are usually represented symbolically by a letter such as f or g. For convenience, *function notation* is often used in calculus. In terms of the definition above, if f is a function and $x \varepsilon A$, then $f(x)$ is the unique number in B corresponding to x.

It is not uncommon to use a letter that reminds us of what a function represents. Thus for example, $A(x)$ may be used to represent the area of a square whose side is x or $V(r)$ may represent the volume of a sphere whose radius is r.

EXAMPLE 2

Suppose f represents the "squaring" function, i.e., the function that squares x. We write

$$f(x) = x^2$$

To compute the value of this function for a particular value of x, simply replace x by that value wherever it appears in the definition of the function.

$$f(3) = 3^2 = 9$$
$$f(-5) = (-5)^2 = 25$$
$$f(\pi) = \pi^2$$
$$f(\sqrt{7}) = (\sqrt{7})^2 = 7$$
$$f(a + b) = (a + b)^2 = a^2 + 2ab + b^2$$

The *domain* of a function is the set of numbers for which the function is defined. While polynomials have the set of *all* real numbers as their domain, many functions must, by their very definition, have restricted domains. For example, $f(x) = \sqrt{x}$ has, as its domain, the set of nonnegative real numbers. (The square root of a negative number is undefined.) The domain of $g(x) = 1/x$ is the set of all real numbers except 0.

2

Because of the geometric or physical nature of a problem, many word problems arising from everyday situations involve functions with restricted domains. For example, the squaring function $f(x) = x^2$ discussed in Example 2 allows all real x, but if $f(x)$ represents the area of a square of side x, then negative values make no sense. The domain would be the set of all *nonnegative* real numbers. (We shall see later that it is sometimes desirable to allow 0 as the dimension of a geometric figure, even though a square or rectangle whose side is 0 is difficult to visualize).

Finally, please note that when dealing with problems in elementary calculus, such as those discussed in this book, only functions of a single variable are considered. We may write $A = xy$ to represent the area of a rectangle of width x and length y, but A is not a function of a single variable unless it is expressed in terms of only one variable. Techniques for accomplishing this are discussed in the pages that follow.

Strategy for Extracting Functions

The most important part of obtaining the function is to read and *understand* the problem. Once the problem is understood, and it is clear what is to be found, there are three steps to determining the function.

Step 1
Draw a diagram (if appropriate). Label all quantities, known and unknown, that are relevant.

Step 2
Write an equation representing the quantity to be expressed as a function. This quantity will usually be represented in terms of two or more variables.

Step 3
Use any constraints specified in the problem to eliminate *all but one* independent variable. A constraint defines a relationship between variables in the problem. The procedure is not complete until only *one* independent variable remains.

Number Problems

Although number problems are relatively simple, they illustrate the above steps quite clearly.

EXAMPLE 3

The sum of two numbers is 40. Express their product as a function of one of the numbers.

Solution

Step 1

In most number problems a diagram is not called for. We label the numbers using the variables x and y.

Let x be the first number

y be the second number

Step 2

We wish to express the product P as a function, so $P = xy$.

Step 3

Since $x + y = 40$, $y = 40 - x$. We substitute into the equation involving P obtained in step 2 and express using function notation.

$$P(x) = x(40 - x)$$
$$P(x) = 40x - x^2$$

EXAMPLE 4

The product of two numbers is 32. Find a function that represents the sum of their squares.

Solution

Step 1

Let x be the first number and y the second.

Step 2

$S = x^2 + y^2$

Step 3

Since $xy = 32$, $y = \dfrac{32}{x}$. It follows that $S(x) = x^2 + \left(\dfrac{32}{x}\right)^2$.

Two-Dimensional Geometry Problems

Most geometry problems are composed of rectangles, triangles, and circles. It is therefore useful to review the formulas for the perimeter and area of these standard geometric shapes.

A *rectangle* of length l and width w has a perimeter equal to the sum of the lengths of its four sides. Its area is the product of its length and width.

$$P = 2l + 2w$$
$$A = lw$$

A special case arises when l and w are equal. The resulting figure is a *square*, whose side is s.

$$P = 4s$$
$$A = s^2$$

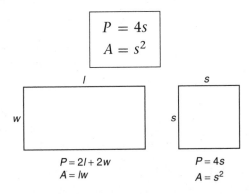

$$P = 2l + 2w$$
$$A = lw$$

$$P = 4s$$
$$A = s^2$$

A *triangle* with base b and altitude h has an area of $\frac{1}{2}bh$. Special cases include right triangles and equilateral triangles. One often encounters triangles where two sides and their included angle are known.

$A = \dfrac{1}{2}bh$	General formula for all triangles
$A = \dfrac{1}{2}ab$	Right triangle whose legs are a and b
$A = \dfrac{\sqrt{3}}{4}s^2$	Equilateral triangle of side s
$A = \dfrac{1}{2}ab \sin\theta$	If two sides and the included angle are known

The perimeter of a triangle is the sum of the lengths of its 3 sides. The perimeter of an equilateral triangle of side s is simply $3s$.

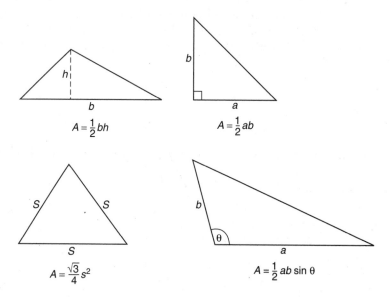

$$A = \frac{1}{2}bh$$

$$A = \frac{1}{2}ab$$

$$A = \frac{\sqrt{3}}{4}s^2$$

$$A = \frac{1}{2}ab\sin\theta$$

A *circle* is measured by its radius r. The perimeter of a circle is known as its *circumference*. Occasionally the diameter d will be given in place of the radius. Since $r = \frac{d}{2}$, the area and circumference may also be expressed in terms of d.

$$C = 2\pi r = \pi d$$
$$A = \pi r^2 = \frac{\pi d^2}{4}$$

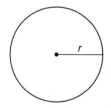

$$C = 2\pi r = \pi d$$
$$A = \pi r^2 = \frac{\pi d^2}{4}$$

EXAMPLE 5

A farmer has 1500 feet of fencing in his barn. He wishes to enclose a rectangular pen, subdivided into two regions by a section of fence down the middle, parallel to one side of the rectangle. Express the area enclosed by the pen as a function of its width x. What is the domain of the function?

Solution

Step 1
We draw a simple diagram, labeling the dimensions of the rectangle.

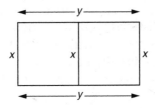

Step 2
We express the area of the rectangle in terms of the variables x and y. Observe that the area of the pen is determined by its *outer* dimensions only; the inner section has no affect on the area.

$$A = xy$$

Step 3
We use the constraint of 1500 feet of fence to obtain a relationship between x and y.

$$3x + 2y = 1500$$

Next we solve for y in terms of x.

$$2y = 1500 - 3x$$

$$y = 750 - \frac{3}{2}x$$

7

Finally, we substitute this expression for y into the area equation obtained in step 2.

$$A = xy$$

$$A = x\left(750 - \frac{3}{2}x\right)$$

$$A(x) = 750x - \frac{3}{2}x^2$$

Mathematically, the domain of $A(x)$ is the set of *all* real numbers. However, in this problem, as with all geometry problems, negative dimensions are unrealistic. Although $x = 0$ may appear to be unrealistic as well, we generally allow a rectangle of zero width or length with the understanding that its area is 0. Such a rectangle is called a *degenerate* rectangle. Since the perimeter is fixed, y gets smaller as x gets larger so the largest value of x occurs when $y = 0$.

$$3x + 2y = 1500$$

$$3x = 1500 \qquad (y = 0)$$

$$x = 500$$

The function describing the area of the farmer's pen is

$$A(x) = 750x - \frac{3}{2}x^2 \qquad 0 \le x \le 500$$

EXAMPLE 6

A piece of wire 12 inches long is to be used to form a square and/or a circle. Determine a function that expresses the *combined* area of both figures. What is its domain?

Solution

Step I

Let x be the side of the square and r the radius of the circle. We shall express the area as a function of x.

8

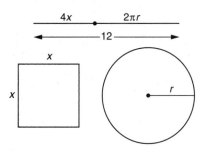

Step 2

$$A = x^2 + \pi r^2$$

Step 3

Since the combined perimeter of the two figures must be 12 inches, we have

$$4x + 2\pi r = 12$$

It follows that

$$2\pi r = 12 - 4x$$

$$r = \frac{12 - 4x}{2\pi} = \frac{6 - 2x}{\pi}$$

Replacing r in terms of x in step 2 gives the area as a function of x.

$$A(x) = x^2 + \pi \left(\frac{6 - 2x}{\pi} \right)^2$$

$$= x^2 + \frac{(6 - 2x)^2}{\pi}$$

If all the wire is used to form the circle, $x = 0$. If all the wire is used for the square, $4x = 12$ and $x = 3$. Our function is

$$A(x) = x^2 + \frac{(6 - 2x)^2}{\pi} \qquad 0 \leq x \leq 3$$

EXAMPLE 7

A 1-mile racetrack has two semicircular ends connected by straight lines. Express the area enclosed by the track as a function of its semicircular radius. Determine its domain.

Solution

Step 1

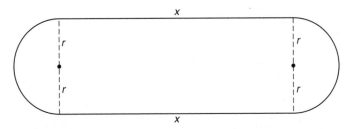

Step 2
The enclosed area consists of a rectangle whose dimensions are x and $2r$ and two semicircles of radius r whose combined area is πr^2.

$$A = 2rx + \pi r^2$$

Step 3
The perimeter of the figure is the length of the two straight sides added to the lengths of the two semicircular arcs. Thus

$$2x + 2\pi r = 1$$
$$2x = 1 - 2\pi r$$
$$x = \frac{1 - 2\pi r}{2}$$

> Each semicircular arc has length πr. Together, they form a complete circle whose circumference is $2\pi r$.

We substitute into the equation obtained in step 2.

$$A(r) = 2r\left(\frac{1 - 2\pi r}{2}\right) + \pi r^2$$
$$= r - 2\pi r^2 + \pi r^2$$
$$= r - \pi r^2$$

Since r cannot be negative, $r \geq 0$. The perimeter of the track

10

is fixed so the maximum value of r occurs when $x = 0$.

$$2x + 2\pi r = 1$$

$$2\pi r = 1 \qquad (x = 0)$$

$$r = \frac{1}{2\pi}$$

The area function and its domain are

$$A(r) = r - \pi r^2 \qquad 0 \le r \le \frac{1}{2\pi}$$

Three–Dimensional Geometry Problems

Most three-dimensional word problems involve boxes, right circular cylinders, spheres, and cones.

A *box* has a volume equal to the product of its length, width, and height. The surface area of a *closed* box is the sum of the areas of its six sides. An *open* box has no top; its volume is the same as for a closed box, but its surface area involves only five sides. A *cube* is a box whose edges are all equal.

Closed box	$V = lwh$	$S = 2lw + 2lh + 2wh$
Open box	$V = lwh$	$S = lw + 2lh + 2wh$
Cube	$V = s^3$	$S = 6s^2$

$V = lwh$
$S = 2lw + 2lh + 2wh$

$V = s^3$
$S = 6s^2$

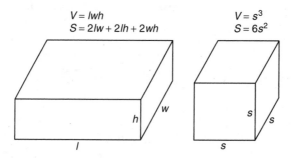

A *right circular cylinder* of length h and radius r has volume $\pi r^2 h$ and *lateral* surface area $2\pi r h$. An easy way to remember these is to multiply the area and circumference of a circle by h.

Circumference of
  a circle $C = 2\pi r$
Lateral surface area
  of a cylinder $S = 2\pi r h$
	Area of a circle $A = \pi r^2$
	
	Volume of
	  a cylinder $V = \pi r^2 h$

The *total* surface area (including the two circular ends) of a cylinder is $2\pi r h + 2\pi r^2$.

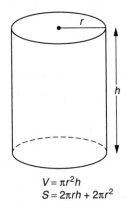

$V = \pi r^2 h$
$S = 2\pi r h + 2\pi r^2$

Cones and spheres are commonly used in word problems. Their volume and surface areas will become familiar with use.

Volume of a sphere	$V = \dfrac{4}{3}\pi r^3$
Surface area of a sphere	$S = 4\pi r^2$
Volume of a cone	$V = \dfrac{\pi}{3} r^2 h$

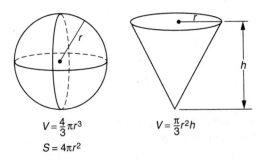

$V = \frac{4}{3}\pi r^3$ $V = \frac{\pi}{3} r^2 h$
$S = 4\pi r^2$

EXAMPLE 8

A closed box has a base twice as long as it is wide. If its volume is 100 in³, express its surface area as a function of the width x of its base.

Solution

Step 1

Since the base of the box is a rectangle whose length is twice its width, we can represent its dimensions by x and $2x$. The height, however, must be represented by a different variable.

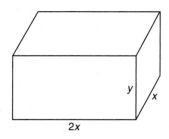

Step 2

The surface area of the box S is the sum of the areas of its six sides. The top and bottom areas are each $2x^2$, the front and back areas are each $2xy$, and the left and right sides each have an area of xy.

$$S = 2x^2 + 2x^2 + 2xy + 2xy + xy + xy$$
$$S = 4x^2 + 6xy$$

Step 3

The volume of the box ($l \times w \times h$), $2x^2y$, is 100 in³.

$$2x^2y = 100$$
$$y = \frac{50}{x^2}$$

Substituting into the result of step 2,

$$S(x) = 4x^2 + 6x\left(\frac{50}{x^2}\right)$$

$$S(x) = 4x^2 + \frac{300}{x}$$

EXAMPLE 9

A cylindrical container with a circular base has a surface area of 64 ft². Express its volume as a function of its radius.

Solution

Step I

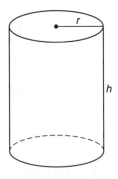

Step 2

$$V = \pi r^2 h$$

Step 3

The surface area of the cylinder is 64 ft². We solve for h in terms of r.

$$2\pi r h + 2\pi r^2 = 64$$

$$2\pi r h = 64 - 2\pi r^2$$

$$h = \frac{64 - 2\pi r^2}{2\pi r}$$

$$h = \frac{32 - \pi r^2}{\pi r}$$

Substituting into the result of step 2, we get

$$V(r) = \pi r^2 \left(\frac{32 - \pi r^2}{\pi r} \right)$$

$$= r(32 - \pi r^2)$$

$$V(r) = 32r - \pi r^3$$

EXAMPLE 10

Water is stored in a tank in the shape of an inverted cone of height 10 ft and diameter 6 ft. Express the volume of water in the tank as a function of the height h of the water level.

Solution

Step 1

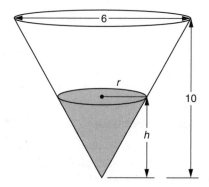

Step 2

The water is in the shape of a cone within the conical tank. Its volume is represented by V.

$$V = \frac{\pi}{3} r^2 h$$

Step 3

To obtain a relationship between r and h we use basic geometry. Viewing the problem from a two-dimensional perspective, we observe two similar triangles: $\triangle ABC$ is similar to $\triangle ADE$.

$$\frac{2r}{h} = \frac{6}{10}$$

$$20r = 6h$$

$$r = \frac{3h}{10}$$

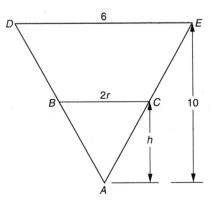

Substituting into the volume equation in step 2, we obtain

$$V(h) = \frac{\pi}{3}\left(\frac{3h}{10}\right)^2 h$$

$$= \frac{\pi}{3} \cdot \frac{9h^2}{100} \cdot h$$

$$V(h) = \frac{3\pi}{100}h^3$$

Business and Economics Problems

Problems arising in business and economics generally deal with money. *Revenue* is the amount of money taken in by a company when selling a product, *cost* is the money paid out by the company for wages, material, rent, and so forth, and *profit* is the difference between revenue and cost. Negative profit indicates a loss.

EXAMPLE 11

A machine can produce 12 clay figures per hour. It costs $750 to set up the machine and $6 per hour to run the machine. Each clay figure requires $2 of material (clay) to produce. If each clay figure will sell for $10, express the revenue, cost, and profit in producing x clay figures as a function of time.

Solution

Step 1

Let x represent the number of clay figures produced and let t represent the number of hours needed to produce them. Let R, C, and P represent the revenue, cost, and profit, respectively.

Step 2

Since each figure sells for $10,

$$R = 10x$$

The cost consists of three parts. Fixed cost is $750, the cost of running the machine for t hours is $6t$ dollars, and the cost of material to produce x figures is $2x$ dollars. Thus

$$C = 750 + 6t + 2x$$

Since Profit = Revenue − Cost

$$
\begin{aligned}
P &= R - C \\
&= 10x - (750 + 6t + 2x) \\
&= 8x - 6t - 750
\end{aligned}
$$

Step 3

Since 12 clay figures are produced per hour, $x = 12t$. Substituting into the results of step 2,

$$R = 10x = 10(12t)$$

$$R(t) = 120t$$

$$C = 750 + 6t + 2x$$

$$= 750 + 6t + 2(12t)$$

$$= 750 + 6t + 24t$$

$$C(t) = 750 + 30t$$

$$P = 8x - 6t - 750$$

$$= 8(12t) - 6t - 750$$

$$= 96t - 6t - 750$$

$$P(t) = 90t - 750$$

EXAMPLE 12

A tour bus has 80 seats. Experience shows that when a tour costs $300, all seats on the bus will be sold. For each additional $10 charged, however, 2 fewer seats will be sold. Find a function that represents the revenue derived from a single bus tour.

Solution

Step 1

In this type of problem it is convenient to let x represent the number of $10 increments above the base price of $300. Thus, for example, if $x = 2$ the price is $320. We let n represent the number of seats sold and p the price per seat.

Step 2

The revenue R is the product of the number of seats sold and the price per seat.

$$R = np$$

Step 3

For each unit increment in x, n decreases by 2 and p increases by 10.

$$n = 80 - 2x$$

$$p = 300 + 10x$$

Substituting into step 2,

$$R = np = (80 - 2x)(300 + 10x)$$

$$R(x) = 24{,}000 + 200x - 20x^2$$

EXAMPLE 13

A river is 100 feet wide. The local telephone company wants to run a cable from point A on one side of the river to a point B on the other side, 500 feet downstream. It costs 3 dollars per foot to run the cable under water while only 2 dollars per foot to run the cable on land. Determine a function representing the total cost to lay the cable.

Solution

Step 1

Let x represent the number of feet from C, directly opposite A, where the cable will emerge from the water, and let y represent the number of feet of cable to be laid under water.

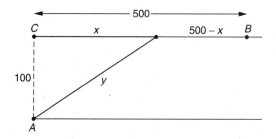

Step 2

The total cost is the sum of the costs to run the cable on land and under water.

$$C = C_{\text{land}} + C_{\text{water}}$$
$$= 2(500 - x) + 3y$$
$$= 1000 - 2x + 3y$$

Step 3

By the Pythagorean theorem, $y = \sqrt{x^2 + 100^2}$, so the total cost function is

$$C(x) = 1000 - 2x + 3\sqrt{x^2 + 10{,}000} \qquad 0 \le x \le 500$$

Supplementary Problems

1. The difference of two numbers is 15. Express their product as a function of the smaller number, x.

2. A rectangle has an area of 200 square meters. Express its perimeter as a function of its width.

3. Caren wants to fence in a rectangular vegetable garden and subdivide it into three regions by using two additional sections of fence parallel to one side, x, of the rectangle. The total enclosed area is to be 1000 ft^2. Express the total length of fencing as a function of x.

4. A rectangle is inscribed in a semicircle of radius 10 with the base of the rectangle lying along the bottom of the semicircle. Express the area of the rectangle as a function of its width and determine its domain.

5. An open box is to be constructed from a rectangular piece of sheet metal 8×12 inches by cutting away identical x-inch squares from each of the four corners and folding up the sides. Express the volume of the resulting box as a function of x.

6. A church window is to be in the shape of a rectangle surmounted by a semicircle. If the perimeter of the window is 100 inches, express its area as a function of its semicircular radius r.

7. An *open* box has a square base. If its surface area is 200 cm^2, express its volume as a function of its base dimension x.

8. A right circular cylinder is inscribed in a sphere of radius 10. Express its volume and surface area as functions of its height h.

9. If 500 apple trees are planted in an orchard, each tree will produce 800 apples. For each additional tree planted, the number of apples produced per tree diminishes by 20. Find a function that represents the total number of apples produced in the orchard.

10. It costs $800 to manufacture a certain model of personal computer. Overhead and other fixed costs to the company are $2000 per week. The wholesale price of a computer is $1500 but, as an incentive, the company will reduce the price of every computer by an additional $10 for each computer purchased in excess of 10. (Thus if 13 computers are purchased, each will cost $1470.) Express the company's weekly profit as a function of the number of computers sold.

Solutions to Supplementary Problems

1. Let x = the smaller number and y = the larger number. Their product is $P = xy$. Since $y - x = 15$, $y = x + 15$. By substitution,

    $$P(x) = x(x + 15)$$
    $$P(x) = x^2 + 15x$$

2.

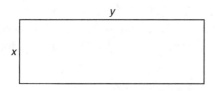

    $P = 2x + 2y$. Since $A = xy = 200$, $y = \dfrac{200}{x}$. By substitution,

    $$P = 2x + 2\left(\frac{200}{x}\right)$$
    $$P(x) = 2x + \frac{400}{x} \qquad x > 0$$

3.

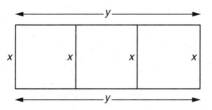

    Let L = length of fence used. $L = 4x + 2y$. The enclosed area, $xy = 1000$, so $y = \dfrac{1000}{x}$. It follows that

    $$L = 4x + 2\left(\frac{1000}{x}\right)$$
    $$L(x) = 4x + \frac{2000}{x} \qquad x > 0$$

4. Let (x, y) represent the point on the circle corresponding to the upper right corner of the rectangle. The length of the rectangle will then be $2x$ and the height y.

21

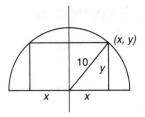

$A = 2xy$. Since $x^2 + y^2 = 100$, $y = \sqrt{100 - x^2}$. By substitution, $A = 2x\sqrt{100 - x^2}$. Since the point on the circle (x, y) was selected in the first quadrant, $0 \le x \le 10$. The area function is

$$A(x) = 2x\sqrt{100 - x^2} \qquad 0 \le x \le 10$$

5. Let l, w, and h represent the length, width, and height, respectively, of the resulting open box. $V = lwh$.

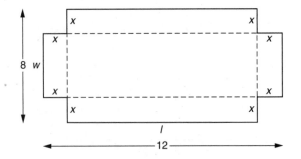

Since the length and width of the box will be the corresponding dimensions of the sheet metal diminished by $2x$, $l = 12 - 2x$, $w = 8 - 2x$, and the height of the box will be just x itself. By substitution,

$$V = (12 - 2x)(8 - 2x)x$$

$$V(x) = 96x - 40x^2 + 4x^3$$

The values of x are restricted by the size of the smaller dimension of the rectangle: $0 \le x \le 4$.

6. If the radius of the semicircle is r, the base of the window will be $2r$. Let x represent the height of the rectangle.

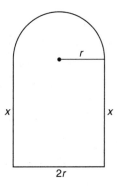

The area of the window is the sum of the areas of the rectangle and semicircle.

$$A = \underbrace{2rx}_{\substack{\text{Area of} \\ \text{rectangle}}} + \underbrace{\tfrac{1}{2}\pi r^2}_{\substack{\text{Area of} \\ \text{semicircle}}}$$

The top of the figure is a semicircle and has a length equal to half the circumference of a full circle. Thus

$$2x + 2r + \pi r = 100$$
$$2x = 100 - 2r - \pi r$$
$$x = 50 - r - \frac{\pi}{2}r$$

$C = 2\pi r$ for a full circle.
$\tfrac{1}{2}C = \pi r.$

Substituting into the area equation,

$$A = 2r\left(50 - r - \frac{\pi}{2}r\right) + \frac{1}{2}\pi r^2$$

$$A = 100r - 2r^2 - \pi r^2 + \frac{1}{2}\pi r^2$$

$$A(r) = 100r - 2r^2 - \frac{1}{2}\pi r^2$$

7. Since the box has a square base, its dimensions are x, x, and y. $V = x^2 y$.

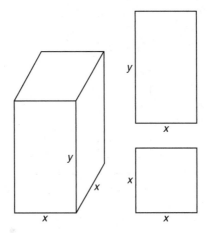

The surface area of the box is the sum of the areas of its five sides. Since the base of the box is a square of side x and each of the four sides is a rectangle x by y, $S = x^2 + 4xy$.

$$\overbrace{x^2}^{\substack{\text{Area} \\ \text{of base}}} + \overbrace{4xy}^{\substack{\text{Area of} \\ \text{4 sides}}} = 200$$

$$4xy = 200 - x^2$$

$$y = \frac{200 - x^2}{4x}$$

Substituting into the volume formula,

$$V = x^2 y$$

$$V(x) = x^2 \left(\frac{200 - x^2}{4x} \right)$$

$$V(x) = x \left(\frac{200 - x^2}{4} \right)$$

$$V(x) = \frac{200x - x^3}{4}$$

8. Let the radius and height of the cylinder be represented by r and h, respectively.

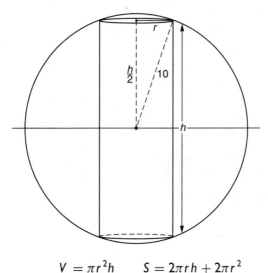

$$V = \pi r^2 h \qquad S = 2\pi r h + 2\pi r^2$$

By the Pythagorean theorem,

$$r^2 + \left(\frac{h}{2}\right)^2 = 10^2$$

$$r^2 + \frac{h^2}{4} = 100$$

$$r^2 = 100 - \frac{h^2}{4}$$

$$r^2 = \frac{400 - h^2}{4}$$

$$r = \frac{\sqrt{400 - h^2}}{2}$$

It follows by substitution that

$$V = \pi \left(\frac{400 - h^2}{4}\right) h \qquad S = 2\pi \left(\frac{\sqrt{400 - h^2}}{2}\right) h + 2\pi \left(\frac{400 - h^2}{4}\right)$$

$$V(h) = \frac{\pi}{4}(400h - h^3) \qquad S(h) = \pi h \sqrt{400 - h^2} + \frac{\pi}{2}(400 - h^2)$$

9. Let x represent the number of trees to be planted *in excess of 500.* Let $N(x)$ represent the number of apples as a function of x. The total number of trees is then $500 + x$ and each tree will produce $800 - 20x$ apples.

Total number of apples
= (number of apples produced by each tree)(number of trees)

$$N(x) = (800 - 20x)(500 + x)$$

$$= 400,000 - 9200x - 20x^2$$

10. Let x represent the number of computers sold. The cost of producing x computers is the sum of the fixed cost and the variable cost.

$$C = \underbrace{2000}_{\text{Fixed cost}} + \underbrace{800x}_{\substack{\text{Cost to make} \\ x \text{ computers}}}$$

If 10 or fewer computers are sold, the price is \$1500 per computer, so the company's revenue $R = 1500x$. The profit,

$$P = R - C$$

$$= 1500x - (2000 + 800x)$$

$$= 700x - 2000$$

If more than 10 computers are sold, the number of computers in excess of 10 is $x - 10$. The price per computer then becomes $1500 - 10(x - 10) = 1600 - 10x$ dollars. In this case the company's revenue becomes $R = (1600 - 10x)x = 1600x - 10x^2$ and the profit

$$P = R - C$$

$$= 1600x - 10x^2 - (2000 + 800x)$$

$$= 800x - 10x^2 - 2000$$

Combining these results,

$$P(x) = \begin{cases} 700x - 2000 & \text{if } x \leq 10 \\ 800x - 10x^2 - 2000 & \text{if } x > 10 \end{cases}$$

Chapter 2

Rates of Change in the Natural and Social Sciences

The average rate of change of a function f with respect to its independent variable x is the quotient $\dfrac{\Delta f(x)}{\Delta x} = \dfrac{f(x+h) - f(x)}{h}$.

The *instantaneous rate of change* is $\lim\limits_{h \to 0} \dfrac{f(x+h) - f(x)}{h}$ which, by definition, is $f'(x)$.

> The instantaneous rate of change of a function with respect to its independent variable is the derivative of the function with respect to that variable.

Most problems dealing with rates of change involve instantaneous rates of change, and the word "instantaneous" is usually omitted. In these problems we simply compute the derivative of the function and evaluate it at the point in question. If the average rate is required, the word "average" will usually be mentioned.

Graphically, the (instantaneous) rate of change of a function is the slope of the tangent line at a point. The average rate of change over an interval is the slope of the secant line connecting the points on the curve corresponding to the endpoints of the interval.

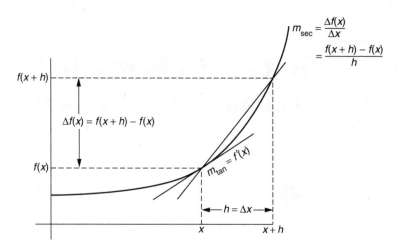

$$m_{sec} = \frac{\Delta f(x)}{\Delta x}$$
$$= \frac{f(x+h) - f(x)}{h}$$

$\Delta f(x) = f(x+h) - f(x)$

$m_{tan} = f'(x)$

$h = \Delta x$

x $x+h$

EXAMPLE I

(a) Find the average rate of change of the area of a square with respect to its side x as x changes from 4 to 7.

(b) Find the rates of change of the area of a square with respect to its side x when $x = 4, 5, 6,$ and 7.

Solution

(a) $A(x) = x^2$. The average rate of change of $A(x)$ with respect to x is $\dfrac{\Delta A(x)}{\Delta x}$.

$$A(x) = x^2$$

$$A(4) = 16 \qquad A(7) = 49$$

$$\Delta A(x) = A(7) - A(4) = 33$$

$$\Delta x = 7 - 4 = 3$$

$$\frac{\Delta A(x)}{\Delta x} = \frac{33}{3} = 11$$

Alternatively,

$$A(x) = x^2, x = 4, h = 3$$

$$\frac{A(x+h) - A(x)}{h} = \frac{A(7) - A(4)}{3} = \frac{49 - 16}{3} = \frac{33}{3} = 11$$

(b) We determine the instantaneous rates of change by computing the derivative of the area function and evaluating it at $x = 4, 5, 6,$ and 7.

$$A(x) = x^2$$
$$A'(x) = 2x$$
$$A'(4) = 8$$
$$A'(5) = 10$$
$$A'(6) = 12$$
$$A'(7) = 14$$

Observe that the area grows at a faster rate as x increases.

EXAMPLE 2

Find the rate of change of the volume of a sphere with respect to its radius when its radius is 5.

Solution

The volume of a sphere of radius r is $V(r) = \frac{4}{3}\pi r^3$.

$$V'(r) = 4\pi r^2$$
$$V'(5) = 100\pi$$

EXAMPLE 3

Let $f(x) = 1/x$. Determine (a) the rate of change of f at $x = 1$ and (b) the average rate of change of f from $x = 1$ to $x = 2$. Interpret the results graphically.

Solution

(a) $f(x) = x^{-1}$

$f'(x) = -x^{-2} = -\dfrac{1}{x^2}$

$f'(1) = -1$

The rate of change is -1.

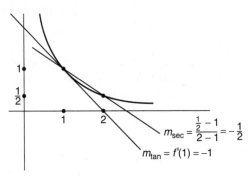

$m_{sec} = \dfrac{\frac{1}{2} - 1}{2 - 1} = -\dfrac{1}{2}$

$m_{tan} = f'(1) = -1$

(b) $x = 1, h = 1$

$$\frac{f(x+h) - f(x)}{h} = \frac{\dfrac{1}{x+h} - \dfrac{1}{x}}{h} = \frac{\dfrac{1}{2} - \dfrac{1}{1}}{1} = -\frac{1}{2}$$

Motion along a Straight Line

Velocity is the rate of change of the position of a moving object with respect to time.

If we are told that a car travels a distance of 100 miles along a straight road, we get a sense of how far the car has traveled but we are given no clue as to *how fast* the car moves. On the other hand, if we are told that the car travels 100 miles in 2 hours, we can judge that the car moved an average of 50 miles per hour. We say that the car's *average* velocity over this 2-hour time interval is 50 mi/h.

The car's average velocity is defined by

$$v_{av} = \frac{\Delta s}{\Delta t}$$

> s represents the car's position relative to a fixed point.

The instantaneous velocity v is defined as the limit of the average velocity, as the length of the time interval approaches 0.

$$v = \lim_{\Delta t \to 0} \frac{\Delta s}{\Delta t}$$

This quantity is the derivative of s with respect to t:

$$v = \frac{ds}{dt}$$

EXAMPLE 4

A bicycle travels along a straight road. At 1:00 it is 1 mile from the end of the road and at 4:00 it is 16 miles from the end of the road. Compute (a) its average velocity from 1:00 to 4:00 and (b) its instantaneous velocity at 3:00.

Solution

(a) Let s represent the bicycle's position relative to the end of the road.

$$v_{av} = \frac{\Delta s}{\Delta t} = \frac{16 - 1}{4 - 1} = \frac{15}{3} = 5 \text{ mi/h}$$

(b) We cannot solve this part of the problem since we do not know the bicycle's location at every point in time. There is not enough information given to compute its instantaneous velocity.

In order to compute instantaneous velocity we need the bicycle's position as a function of time.

EXAMPLE 5

A bicycle travels along a straight road. At t o'clock it is t^2 miles from the end of the road. Compute (a) its average velocity from 1:00 to 4:00 and (b) its instantaneous velocity at 3:00.

Solution

(a) Observe that as far as the average velocity is concerned, the problem is identical to Example 4. If $s = t^2$, when $t = 1$, $s = 1$ and when $t = 4$, $s = 16$.

$$v_{av} = \frac{\Delta s}{\Delta t} = \frac{16 - 1}{4 - 1} = \frac{15}{3} = 5 \text{ mi/h}$$

(*b*) Since the position of the bicycle is known at every point in time, the instantaneous velocity can be computed.
Let $s(t) = t^2$. Then $v(t) = s'(t) = 2t$
At 3 o'clock, $t = 3$ so $v(3) = s'(3) = 6$ mi/h.

The derivative determines the *velocity* of a moving object, which indicates its speed as well as its direction. Often the phrase "how fast" will be used in the formulation of a word problem. "How fast" indicates that only the speed of the object is desired. Unlike velocity, which may be positive, zero, or negative, the speed of a moving object is always nonnegative. Mathematically, speed is the absolute value of velocity:

$$\text{speed} = |\text{velocity}|$$

EXAMPLE 6

A particle's position (in inches) along the x axis after t seconds of travel is given by the equation

$$x = 24t^2 - t^3 + 10$$

(*a*) What is the particle's average velocity during the first 3 seconds of travel?
(*b*) Where is the particle and how fast is it moving after 3 seconds of travel?
(*c*) Where is the particle and how fast is it moving after 20 seconds of travel?
(*d*) When is the velocity of the particle 0? What is the particle's position at that instant?
(*e*) Describe the motion of the particle during the first 20 seconds of travel.

Solution

(*a*) The particle's position when $t = 0$ is $x = 10$ inches. When $t = 3$, $x = 199$ inches.

$$v_{av} = \frac{\Delta x}{\Delta t} = \frac{199 - 10}{3 - 0} = \frac{189}{3} = 63 \text{ in/sec}$$

32

(b) When $t = 3$, its position $x = 199$. The particle's instantaneous velocity is determined using the derivative.

$$v = \frac{dx}{dt} = 48t - 3t^2$$

When $t = 3$, $v = 117$ in/sec. Since this is a positive number, it represents the speed as well.

(c) When $t = 20$, its position $x = 24(20)^2 - 20^3 + 10 = 1610$. Its velocity,

$$v = \frac{dx}{dt} = 48t - 3t^2$$

When $t = 20$, $v = -240$ in/sec. The negative velocity indicates that the particle is moving in the negative direction. The speed of the particle is 240 in/sec.

(d)
$$v = 48t - 3t^2$$
$$0 = 48t - 3t^2$$
$$0 = 3t(16 - t)$$
$$t = 0 \qquad t = 16$$

The velocity of the particle is 0 when $t = 0$ and when $t = 16$. When $t = 0$, $x = 10$ and when $t = 16$, $x = 2058$.

(e) The particle begins at rest at $x = 10$. For the first 16 seconds, the particle has a positive velocity and moves in the positive direction. When $t = 16$, the particle stops momentarily ($v = 0$) at $x = 2058$. It then moves in the negative direction and returns to $x = 1610$ when $t = 20$.

The *acceleration* of a moving object is the rate of change of its velocity with respect to time. Thus $a(t) = v'(t)$. If $s(t)$ represents the position of the particle at time t, then $a(t) = s''(t)$.

EXAMPLE 7

Compute the acceleration of the particle in Example 6 at times $t = 3, 5, 10$, and 15.

33

Solution

Since $v(t) = 48t - 3t^2$, $a(t) = v'(t) = 48 - 6t$.

When $t = 3$, $a = 30$ in/sec^2

When $t = 5$, $a = 18$ in/sec^2

When $t = 10$, $a = -12$ in/sec^2

When $t = 15$, $a = -42$ in/sec^2

> Since the units of velocity in this example are inches per second, the units of acceleration would be inches per second per second. This is usually written in/sec/sec or in/sec^2. Other common units of acceleration are ft/sec^2, mi/h^2, and meters/sec^2.

EXAMPLE 8

The height (in feet) at any time t (in seconds) of a projectile thrown vertically is

$$h(t) = -16t^2 + 256t$$

(a) What is the projectile's average velocity for the first 5 seconds of travel?

(b) How fast is the projectile traveling 6 seconds after it is thrown? How high is it?

(c) How fast is the projectile traveling 10 seconds after it is thrown? How high is it?

(d) When is the maximum height reached by the projectile? What is its maximum height?

(e) When does the projectile return to the ground and with what velocity?

(f) Describe the motion of the projectile.

Solution

(a) $h(t) = -16t^2 + 256t$. When $t = 0$, $h = 0$ and when $t = 5$, $h = -16(5)^2 + 256(5) = 880$ ft.

$$v_{av} = \frac{\Delta h}{\Delta t} = \frac{880 - 0}{5 - 0} = 176 \text{ ft/sec}$$

(b) Since we are looking for the instantaneous velocity we compute the derivative $\frac{dh}{dt}$. $v = \frac{dh}{dt} = -32t + 256$. When

34

$t = 6, v = -32(6) + 256 = 64$ ft/sec. The height of the projectile when $t = 6$ is $h = -16(6)^2 + 256(6) = 960$ ft.

(c) $v = \dfrac{dh}{dt} = -32t + 256$. When $t = 10, v = -64$ ft/sec. The negative velocity indicates that the projectile is moving in the negative direction (downward) at a speed of 64 ft/sec. The height of the projectile when $t = 10$ is $h = -16(10)^2 + 256(10) = 960$ ft.

(d)
$$v = -32t + 256$$
$$0 = -32t + 256 \qquad \leftarrow \text{Maximum height is reached when } v = 0$$
$$32t = 256$$
$$t = 8 \text{ sec}$$
$$h_{max} = -16(8)^2 + 256(8) \qquad \leftarrow \text{Maximum height is reached after 8 sec}$$
$$= 1024 \text{ feet}$$

(e) The projectile returns to the ground when $h = 0$.

$$h(t) = -16t^2 + 256t$$
$$0 = -16t^2 + 256t$$
$$0 = -16t(t - 16)$$
$$t = 0 \qquad t = 16$$

Since the ball was thrown at time $t = 0$, the ball returns to the ground after 16 seconds. Its velocity at this time, from the velocity function $v(t) = -32t + 256$ is

$$v(16) = -32(16) + 256 = -256 \text{ ft/sec}$$

The negative velocity indicates that the ball is traveling downward at a speed of 256 ft/sec when it hits the ground.

(f) When $t = 0, h = 0$ (the projectile is at ground level) and $v = 256$ ft/sec. This is the *initial velocity*. As t increases, the height h increases and the velocity v decreases, reaching a value of 0 when $t = 8$ sec. At this point the maximum height of the projectile is reached, 1024 ft. As t increases past 8 sec, v becomes negative and h gets

35

smaller, indicating that the projectile is returning to the ground. The projectile returns to the ground after 16 sec.

Applications to Science and Engineering

EXAMPLE 9

The linear density of a rod is the rate of change of its mass with respect to its length. A nonhomogeneous rod has a length of 9 feet and a total mass of 24 slugs. If the mass of a section of the rod of length x (measured from its leftmost end) is proportional to the square root of this length,

(*a*) Compute the average density of the rod.
(*b*) Determine the density function and compute the density of the rod 4 ft from its leftmost end.

Solution

We let $m(x)$ represent the mass of the section of the rod of length x measured from its leftmost end. The description of the problem tells us that $m(x) = k\sqrt{x}$. Since the total mass of the rod is 24 slugs, $m(9) = 24$.

$$m(9) = 24$$

$$k\sqrt{9} = 24$$

$$3k = 24$$

$$k = 8$$

Thus $m(x) = 8\sqrt{x}$.

(*a*) The average density is $\dfrac{m(9) - m(0)}{9 - 0} = \dfrac{24 - 0}{9} = \dfrac{8}{3}$ slugs/ft

(*b*) We represent the density function by $\rho(x)$. $\rho(x) = m'(x)$.

$$m(x) = 8\sqrt{x} = 8x^{1/2}$$

36

$$\rho(x) = m'(x) = 4x^{-1/2} = \frac{4}{\sqrt{x}}$$

$$\rho(4) = 2 \text{ slugs/ft}$$

The movement of electrons through a wire produces an electric current. If Q is the charge flowing through the wire measured in coulombs, then the current I, measured in amperes, is the rate of change of Q with respect to time in seconds.

EXAMPLE 10

The charge in coulombs that passes through a wire after t seconds is given by the function

$$Q(t) = t^3 - 2t^2 + 5t + 2$$

(a) Determine the average current during the first two seconds.

(b) Determine the current at the end of two seconds.

Solution

(a) $I_{av} = \dfrac{\Delta Q}{\Delta t} = \dfrac{Q(2) - Q(0)}{2 - 0} = \dfrac{12 - 2}{2} = 5$ amperes

(b) $I(t) = Q'(t) = 3t^2 - 4t + 5$
$I(2) = 3(2)^2 - 4(2) + 5 = 9$ amperes

EXAMPLE 11

The number of bacteria in a Petri dish after t hours is $n(t) = 2t^3 + 5t^2 + t + 2$. How fast is the population growing after 3 hours?

Solution

$$\frac{dn}{dt} = 6t^2 + 10t + 1$$

When $t = 3$, $dn/dt = 85$. The bacteria are growing at the rate of 85 per hour.

37

EXAMPLE 12

An 1800-gallon tank of water drains from the bottom in 30 minutes. According to Torricelli's law, the volume of water remaining in the tank after t minutes is

$$V = 1800\left(1 - \frac{t}{30}\right)^2 \qquad 0 \le t \le 30$$

How fast is the water draining from the tank after 20 minutes?

Solution

$$\frac{dV}{dt} = 3600\left(1 - \frac{t}{30}\right)\left(-\frac{1}{30}\right)$$

$$= -120\left(1 - \frac{t}{30}\right)$$

When $t = 20$

$$\frac{dV}{dt} = -120\left(1 - \frac{20}{30}\right) = -40 \text{ gallons per minute}$$

Water is draining at the rate of 40 gallons per minute. The negative sign indicates that the volume of water is getting smaller.

EXAMPLE 13

An environmental study of a small town indicates that in t years the level of carbon monoxide will be $q(t) = 0.005t^3 + 0.02t^2 + 0.01t + 2.5$ parts per million (ppm). At what rate will the CO level be increasing 1 and 2 years from now?

Solution

The rate of change of the CO level after t years is
$q'(t) = 0.015t^2 + 0.04t + 0.01$
After 1 year $q'(1) = 0.015 + 0.04 + 0.01 = 0.065$ ppm per year
After 2 years $q'(2) = 0.06 + 0.08 + 0.01 = 0.15$ ppm per year

38

Business and Economics

The *marginal cost* of producing an item is the rate at which its cost changes with respect to the number of items produced. Thus if $C(x)$ is the cost of producing x items, the marginal cost is $C'(x)$.

The marginal cost approximates the additional cost necessary to produce one additional item. Thus $C'(x)$ is the approximate cost incurred to produce the $(x + 1)$st item.

Similarly, if $R(x)$ and $P(x)$ represent the revenue and profit, respectively, in selling a quantity of x units, then $R'(x)$ represents *marginal revenue* and $P'(x)$ the *marginal profit*.

EXAMPLE 14

Suppose the total cost of producing x items is given by the function

$$C(x) = 0.001x^3 + 0.025x^2 + 3x + 5$$

Compute the marginal cost of producing the 51st item.

Solution

Since $C'(x)$ is the approximate cost incurred to produce the $(x + 1)$st item we need to compute $C'(50)$.

$$C'(x) = 0.003x^2 + 0.05x + 3$$

$$C'(50) = 0.003(50)^2 + 0.05(50) + 3$$

$$= 7.50 + 2.50 + 3$$

$$= \$13.00$$

The marginal cost is $13.00. For comparison, the exact cost to produce the 51st item is

$$C(51) - C(50) = [0.001(51)^3 + 0.025(51)^2 + 3(51) + 5]$$

$$-[0.001(50)^3 + 0.025(50)^2 + 3(50) + 5]$$

$$= 355.676 - 342.50$$

$$= \$13.176$$

EXAMPLE 15

The value of a machine after t years of service is $V(t) = 100t^2 - 3000t + 20,000$ dollars. At what rate does the machine depreciate after 5 years?

Solution

The rate of depreciation is the rate at which value is lost. If $V(t)$ represents the value of the machine after t years, $V'(t)$ represents the rate at which its value changes.

$$V'(t) = 200t - 3000$$
$$V'(5) = -2000$$

The machine depreciates at the rate of $2000 per year after 5 years.

Supplementary Problems

1. A closed box with a square base has a volume of 100 in^3. Compute the rate of change of its surface area with respect to its base dimension x when $x = 5$.
2. If $f(x) = \sqrt{x}$, determine
   (a) the rate of change of f with respect to x when $x = 16$
   (b) the average rate of change of f from $x = 16$ to $x = 25$
3. The position of a moving object after t minutes of travel is $s(t) = 2t^3 - 27t^2 + 84t + 25$ feet.
   (a) What is the object's average velocity during the first 2 minutes?
   (b) Where is the object and how fast is it moving after 1 minute of travel? 5 minutes? 10 minutes?
   (c) What is the acceleration of the object after 1 minute? 5 minutes? 10 minutes?
   (d) When is the velocity of the object 0? What is the object's position at that time?
   (e) Describe the motion of the object during the first 10 minutes of travel.
4. The height after t seconds of travel of a projectile thrown upward from the top of a 96-ft building is $h(t) = 80t - 16t^2 + 96$ ft.

(a) What is the projectile's average velocity for the first 2 seconds of travel?

(b) What is the projectile's initial velocity?

(c) What is the projectile's velocity after 5 seconds? What is its position?

(d) What is the maximum height reached by the projectile?

(e) When does the projectile hit the ground and with what velocity does it hit?

5. A rod of length 5 ft has a linear density proportional to the cube of the distance from one end. If the total mass of the rod is 500 slugs, compute

(a) The average density of the rod

(b) The density of the rod at its midpoint

6. Boyle's law states that when a gas is compressed at constant temperature, the product of its pressure and volume remains constant. If the pressure of a gas is 80 lb/in^2 when the volume is 40 in^3, find the rate of change of pressure with respect to volume when the volume is 20 in^3.

7. If x items of a commodity are sold to a wholesaler, the price per item is $500 - 2x - 0.1x^2$ dollars. Compute the marginal revenue derived from the sale of the 11th unit.

Solutions to Supplementary Problems

1.

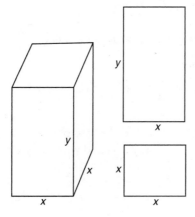

The surface area of the box is the sum of the areas of its six sides.

$$S = 2x^2 + 4xy$$

Since its volume is 100 in³, $x^2y = 100$ and $y = \dfrac{100}{x^2}$. It follows that

$$S(x) = 2x^2 + 4x \cdot \frac{100}{x^2}$$
$$S(x) = 2x^2 + 400x^{-1}$$

Differentiating,

$$S'(x) = 4x - 400x^{-2}$$
$$= 4x - \frac{400}{x^2}$$

The rate of change is determined by letting $x = 5$.

$$S'(5) = 20 - \frac{400}{25} = 4$$

2. (a) The rate of change of f is the value of its derivative at $x = 16$.

$$f(x) = \sqrt{x} = x^{1/2}$$
$$f'(x) = \frac{1}{2}x^{-1/2} = \frac{1}{2x^{1/2}} = \frac{1}{2\sqrt{x}}$$
$$f'(16) = \frac{1}{8}$$

(b) The average rate of change is the value $\dfrac{f(x+h) - f(x)}{h}$ where $x = 16$ and $h = 9$.

$$\frac{f(x+h) - f(x)}{h} = \frac{f(25) - f(16)}{9} = \frac{5 - 4}{9} = \frac{1}{9}$$

Alternatively, if $y = \sqrt{x}$, the rate of change is $\Delta y / \Delta x$. When $x = 16$, $y = 4$ and when $x = 25$, $y = 5$.

$$\frac{\Delta y}{\Delta x} = \frac{5 - 4}{25 - 16} = \frac{1}{9}$$

3. (a) When $t = 0$, $s = 25$ and when $t = 2$, $s = 101$

$$v_{av} = \frac{\Delta s}{\Delta t} = \frac{101 - 25}{2 - 0} = 38 \text{ ft/min}$$

(b)
$$s = 2t^3 - 27t^2 + 84t + 25$$

$$v = \frac{ds}{dt} = 6t^2 - 54t + 84$$

When $t = 1, s = 84$ ft and $v = 36$ ft/min
When $t = 5, s = 20$ ft and $v = -36$ ft/min
When $t = 10, s = 165$ ft and $v = 144$ ft/min

(c) $a = \frac{dv}{dt} = 12t - 54$
When $t = 1, a = -42$ ft/min^2
When $t = 5, a = 6$ ft/min^2
When $t = 10, a = 66$ ft/min^2

(d) From part (b) $v = 6t^2 - 54t + 84$. Let $v = 0$ and solve for t.

$$0 = 6t^2 - 54t + 84$$

$$0 = 6(t - 2)(t - 7)$$

$$t = 2 \qquad t = 7$$

The position of the object at these times is determined from the position function. When $t = 2, s = 101$ and when $t = 7$, $s = -24$.

(e) The object begins moving when $t = 0$. Its position at this time is $s = 25$. During the first 2 minutes of travel ($0 \le t \le 2$), it moves in the positive direction until its position $s = 101$. For the next 5 minutes ($2 \le t \le 7$) its velocity is negative so the object moves in the negative direction until its position becomes $s = -24$. The velocity then becomes positive again and for the next 3 minutes ($7 \le t \le 10$) it moves in the positive direction until its position is $s = 165$.

4. (a) $h(t) = 80t - 16t^2 + 96$
$h(0) = 96$
$h(2) = 192$

$$v_{av} = \frac{h(2) - h(0)}{2 - 0} = \frac{192 - 96}{2 - 0} = 48 \text{ ft/sec}$$

(b) $v(t) = h'(t) = 80 - 32t$
$v(0) = 80$ ft/sec

(c) $v(t) = h'(t) = 80 - 32t$
$v(5) = -80$ ft/sec
$h(5) = 96$ ft

After 5 seconds the projectile has returned to the same height from which it was thrown The velocity is negative since it is on its way down.

43

(d) The maximum height is reached when the projectile's velocity is 0.

$$v(t) = 80 - 32t$$

$$0 = 80 - 32t$$

$$t = \frac{80}{32} = \frac{5}{2}$$

$$h(5/2) = 196 \text{ ft}$$

The maximum height reached is 196 ft above the ground.

(e) The projectile returns to the ground when $h(t) = 0$.

$$h(t) = 80t - 16t^2 + 96$$

$$0 = 80t - 16t^2 + 96$$

$$0 = 5t - t^2 + 6$$

$$0 = -(t^2 - 5t - 6)$$

$$0 = -(t - 6)(t + 1)$$

$$t = -1 \qquad t = 6$$

We reject the first solution. The projectile hits the ground 6 seconds after it is thrown.

$$v(6) = 80 - 32 \cdot 6 = -112 \text{ ft/sec}$$

5. Let $m(x)$ represent the mass of the rod from its end until point x. Then $m(x) = kx^3$. Since the total mass is 500 slugs,

$$m(5) = 500$$

$$k \cdot 5^3 = 500$$

$$k = 4$$

Therefore, $m(x) = 4x^3$

(a) $m(0) = 0$ and $m(5) = 500$

$$\rho_{av} = \frac{m(5) - m(0)}{5 - 0} = \frac{500 - 0}{5 - 0} = 100 \text{ slugs/ft}$$

(b) $\rho(x) = m'(x) = 12x^2$

$\rho(2.5) = 75$ slugs/ft

6. Boyle's law may be stated $PV = C$. Since $P = 80$ when $V = 40$, $C = 80 \cdot 40 = 3200$.

$$PV = 3200$$

$$P = \frac{3200}{V}$$

$$= 3200V^{-1}$$

$$\frac{dP}{dV} = -3200V^{-2}$$

$$= -\frac{3200}{V^2}$$

When $V = 20$, $\dfrac{dP}{dV} = -\dfrac{3200}{20^2} = -8$ lb/in^2 per in^3

7. Since revenue = (number of items sold)(price per item),

$$R(x) = (500 - 2x - 0.1x^2)x$$

$$= 500x - 2x^2 - 0.1x^3$$

$$R'(x) = 500 - 4x - 0.3x^2$$

$$R'(10) = 500 - 40 - 30$$

$$= 430$$

The marginal revenue derived from the sale of the 11th unit is $430.

Chapter 3

Related Rates

In Chapter 2 we discussed the *rate of change of a function*. It is not uncommon for a problem to involve several rates of change. *Related rates* problems are concerned with the relationships between several variables and how the rate of change of one affects the rate of change of another.

In this chapter we consider related rates problems involving algebraic functions. Problems involving trigonometric functions are considered in Chapter 6.

The predominant tool used in the solution of related rates problems is the chain rule. Since most related rates problems deal with time as the independent variable, we state the chain rule in terms of t:

$$\frac{dy}{dt} = \frac{dy}{dx} \cdot \frac{dx}{dt}$$

Before we discuss how to solve related rates problems, let's review some important implications of the chain rule.

EXAMPLE I

Compute the derivative of x^3 with respect to t.

Solution

The derivative of x^3 with respect to x is $3x^2$. However, its derivative *with respect to t* is somewhat different. To understand what it is, let $y = x^3$.

$$\frac{dy}{dt} = \frac{dy}{dx} \cdot \frac{dx}{dt}$$

$$= 3x^2 \frac{dx}{dt}$$

Thus the derivative of x^3 with respect to t, $\frac{d}{dt}(x^3)$, is $3x^2\frac{dx}{dt}$. Unless we know the relationship between x and t we cannot simplify any further.

The result of Example 1 can be stated in a more general form.

$$\boxed{\frac{d}{dt}f(x) = f'(x)\frac{dx}{dt}}$$

Of course, the argument of f will not always be x, but the *independent* variable is usually t in a related rates problem.

EXAMPLE 2

$$\frac{d}{dt}(w^5) = 5w^4\frac{dw}{dt} \qquad \frac{d}{dt}\left(\frac{1}{y}\right) = -\frac{1}{y^2}\frac{dy}{dt} \qquad \frac{d}{dt}(\sqrt{z}) = \frac{1}{2\sqrt{z}}\frac{dz}{dt}$$

The following example illustrates the use of the chain rule. Although not a word problem, it will help clarify basic ideas.

EXAMPLE 3

If $y = x^3 + 4x^2$ and $\frac{dx}{dt} = 3$, compute $\frac{dy}{dt}$ when $x = 1$.

    Solution

$$\frac{dy}{dt} = \frac{d}{dt}(x^3 + 4x^2)$$

$$= (3x^2 + 8x)\frac{dx}{dt}$$

Since $\dfrac{dx}{dt} = 3$,

$$\frac{dy}{dt} = (3x^2 + 8x) \cdot 3$$

Even though $\dfrac{dx}{dt}$ is constant, $\dfrac{dy}{dt}$ changes as x changes. When $x = 1$

$$\frac{dy}{dt} = 11 \cdot 3 = 33$$

In solving word problems, the following steps should be followed:

Step 1
Draw a diagram (if applicable). Label all variables with an appropriate symbol. Label constants with their numerical values.

Step 2
Determine which rates are given and which rate you need to find. Write them down for future reference.

Step 3
Find an equation (or several equations) relating the variables defined in step 1.

Step 4
Differentiate the equation(s) in step 3 with respect to time.

Step 5
Substitute all given information into the result of step 4 and solve for the unknown rate. Insert appropriate units.

The basic technique is illustrated in the next example.

EXAMPLE 4

A ladder 20 feet long is placed against a wall. The foot of the ladder begins to slide away from the wall at the rate of 1 ft/sec. How fast is the top of the ladder sliding down the wall when the foot of the ladder is 12 feet from the wall?

48

Solution

Step 1

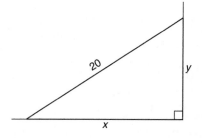

Step 2

Given: $\dfrac{dx}{dt} = 1$

← Since x is increasing, dx/dt is positive, even though the foot of the ladder is moving to the left.

Find: $\dfrac{dy}{dt}$ when $x = 12$

Step 3

Observing a right triangle, we use the theorem of Pythagoras to obtain a relationship between x and y:

$$x^2 + y^2 = 20^2$$

Step 4

Differentiate with respect to t:

$$\frac{d}{dt}x^2 + \frac{d}{dt}y^2 = \frac{d}{dt}400$$

$$2x\frac{dx}{dt} + 2y\frac{dy}{dt} = 0 \qquad \text{← Divide by 2 for convenience}$$

$$x\frac{dx}{dt} + y\frac{dy}{dt} = 0$$

Step 5

We know from step 2 that $dx/dt = 1$ and we know that $x = 12$ at the instant in question. Before we can compute dy/dt, however, we need to find y at this instant. This is

49

accomplished by using the equation obtained in step 3.

$$x^2 + y^2 = 20^2$$

$$12^2 + y^2 = 20^2$$

$$144 + y^2 = 400$$

> If you recognize a 12-16-20 right triangle, this calculation is unnecessary.

$$y^2 = 256$$

$$y = 16$$

Substituting into the equation obtained in step 4, we obtain

$$12 \cdot 1 + 16\frac{dy}{dt} = 0$$

$$16\frac{dy}{dt} = -12$$

$$\frac{dy}{dt} = -\frac{3}{4}$$

The negative derivative means that y is decreasing. The top of the ladder is *falling* at the rate of $\frac{3}{4}$ ft/sec.

EXAMPLE 5

At a certain instant, car A is 60 miles north of car B. A is traveling south at a rate of 20 mi/h while B is traveling east at 30 mi/h. How fast is the distance between them changing 1 hour later?

Solution

Step I

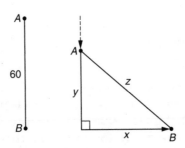

Step 2

Given: $\dfrac{dx}{dt} = 30,$

$\dfrac{dy}{dt} = -20$ ← dy/dt is negative since y is shrinking. If we take $\dfrac{dy}{dt} = 20$, we will get an incorrect answer.

Find: $\dfrac{dz}{dt}$ 1 hour later

Step 3

$$z^2 = x^2 + y^2$$

Step 4

$$2z\frac{dz}{dt} = 2x\frac{dx}{dt} + 2y\frac{dy}{dt}$$

$$z\frac{dz}{dt} = x\frac{dx}{dt} + y\frac{dy}{dt}$$

Step 5

After 1 hour, $x = 30$ miles and $y = 60 - 20 = 40$ miles.

Distance = rate × time

$$z = \sqrt{x^2 + y^2}$$
$$= \sqrt{900 + 1600} = 50 \text{ miles}$$

From step 4

$$50\frac{dz}{dt} = 30 \cdot 30 + 40(-20)$$

$$50\frac{dz}{dt} = 100$$

$$\frac{dz}{dt} = 2$$

The distance between the cars is increasing at the rate of 2 mi/h.

EXAMPLE 6

A plane, P, flies horizontally at an altitude of 2 miles with a speed of 480 mi/h. At a certain moment it passes directly over a radar station, R. How fast is the distance between the plane and the radar station increasing 1 minute later?

Solution

Step 1

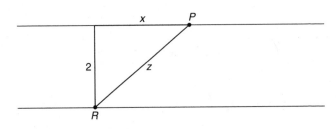

Step 2

Given: $\dfrac{dx}{dt} = 480$

Find: $\dfrac{dz}{dt}$ 1/60 hour later   ← Units of time must be consistent throughout the problem

Step 3

By the theorem of Pythagoras, $z^2 = x^2 + 2^2$.

Step 4

$$2z\frac{dz}{dt} = 2x\frac{dx}{dt} + 0$$

$$z\frac{dz}{dt} = x\frac{dx}{dt}$$

Step 5

Since the plane travels 480 mi/h, it will have flown 8 miles in $\dfrac{1}{60}$ hour $\left(480 \times \dfrac{1}{60} = 8\right)$. Since $x = 8$, the value of z is easily determined by the Pythagorean theorem.

52

$$z^2 = x^2 + 2^2$$
$$= 64 + 4$$
$$= 68$$
$$z = \sqrt{68} = 2\sqrt{17}$$

From step 4,

$$2\sqrt{17}\frac{dz}{dt} = 8 \cdot 480$$

$$\frac{dz}{dt} = \frac{1920}{\sqrt{17}} \text{ mi/h}$$

EXAMPLE 7

A point is moving along the circle $x^2 + y^2 = 25$ in the first quadrant in such a way that its x coordinate changes at the rate of 2 cm/sec. How fast is its y coordinate changing as the point passes through (3, 4)?

Solution

Step 1

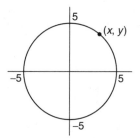

Step 2

Given: $\dfrac{dx}{dt} = 2$ Find: $\dfrac{dy}{dt}$ when $x = 3$ and $y = 4$

Step 3

Since the point must lie on the circle, the relationship between x and y is $x^2 + y^2 = 25$.

53

Step 4

$$2x\frac{dx}{dt} + 2y\frac{dy}{dt} = 0$$

$$x\frac{dx}{dt} + y\frac{dy}{dt} = 0$$

Step 5

$$3 \cdot 2 + 4\frac{dy}{dt} = 0$$

$$\frac{dy}{dt} = -\frac{3}{2} \text{ cm/sec}$$

> Since dx/dt is positive and the point is in the first quadrant, the point is moving along the circle in a clockwise direction. It makes sense that dy/dt is negative, as the point is moving down.

EXAMPLE 8

The dimensions of a rectangle are continuously changing. The width increases at the rate of 3 in/sec while the length decreases at the rate of 2 in/sec. At one instant the rectangle is a 20-inch square. How fast is its area changing 3 seconds later? Is the area increasing or decreasing?

Solution

Step 1

Represent the width and length of the rectangle by x and y, respectively.

Step 2

Given: $\frac{dx}{dt} = 3, \frac{dy}{dt} = -2$ Find: $\frac{dA}{dt}$ 3 seconds later

Step 3
$$A = xy$$

Step 4

We use the product rule to compute $\dfrac{dA}{dt}$. All derivatives are taken with respect to t.

$$\frac{dA}{dt} = x\frac{dy}{dt} + y\frac{dx}{dt}$$

Step 5

3 seconds later, $x = 20 + 3 \cdot 3 = 29$ and $y = 20 + 3(-2) = 14$

$$\frac{dA}{dt} = 29 \cdot (-2) + 14 \cdot 3 = -16$$

Since $\dfrac{dA}{dt}$ is negative, the area is *decreasing* at the rate of 16 in^2/sec.

EXAMPLE 9

A trough filled with water is 2 m long and has a cross section in the shape of an isosceles trapezoid 30 cm wide at the bottom, 60 cm wide at the top, and a height of 50 cm. If the trough leaks water at the rate of 2000 cm^3/min, how fast is the water level falling when the water is 20 cm deep?

Solution

Step 1

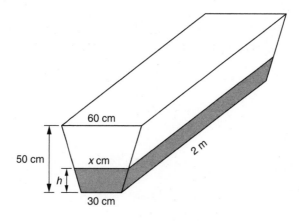

Step 2
Let V represent the volume of water in the tank.

Given: $\dfrac{dV}{dt} = -2000$ ← *dV/dt is negative since the volume of water in the trough is getting smaller.*

Find: $\dfrac{dh}{dt}$ when $h = 20$

> The area of a trapezoid is $\dfrac{h}{2}(a + b)$

Step 3

The cross-sectional area of the water is $A = \dfrac{h}{2}(x + 30)$. The volume of water $V = l \times A$. l is the length of the trough so $V = l \cdot \dfrac{h}{2}(x + 30)$. Since the units in the problem must be consistent, we take $l = 200$ cm. Thus $V = 100h(x + 30)$. Since x is not mentioned in either the "Given" or the "Find" in step 2, we should eliminate x from this equation. To accomplish this, we observe similar triangles.

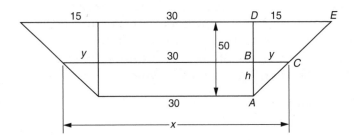

In this figure $\triangle ABC$ is similar to $\triangle ADE$. Since their corresponding sides are proportional,

$$\frac{y}{15} = \frac{h}{50}$$

$$y = \frac{3}{10}h$$

Since $x = 2y + 30$ (see diagram), it follows that $x = \dfrac{3}{5}h + 30$ and

$$V = 100h(x + 30)$$

$$= 100h\left(\frac{3}{5}h + 60\right)$$

$$V = 60h^2 + 6000h$$

Step 4

$$\frac{dV}{dt} = (120h + 6000)\frac{dh}{dt}$$

Step 5

We substitute $\dfrac{dV}{dt} = -2000$ and $h = 20$ into the result of step 4.

$$-2000 = 8400\frac{dh}{dt}$$

$$\frac{dh}{dt} = -\frac{2000}{8400} = -\frac{5}{21} \text{ cm/min}$$

The minus sign indicates that the water level is *falling* at the rate of $\dfrac{5}{21}$ cm/min.

EXAMPLE 10

Water is being pumped into a conical tank at the rate of 100 ft³/min. The height of the tank is 20 ft and its radius is 5 ft. How fast is the water level rising when the water height is 10 ft?

Solution

Step 1

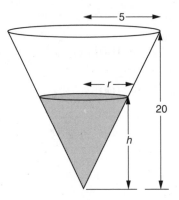

Step 2

Let V represent the volume of water in the tank. The volume is increasing at the rate of 100 ft³/min.

Given: $\dfrac{dV}{dt} = 100$ Find: $\dfrac{dh}{dt}$ when $h = 10$

Step 3

The relationship between V, r, and h is given by the formula for the volume of a cone:

$$V = \frac{\pi}{3}r^2h$$

Since we are given no information about r or dr/dt, it is best to eliminate r from this equation. This is accomplished by observing the cone from a two-dimensional perspective. By observing that $\triangle ABC$ is similar to $\triangle ADE$ in the diagram to the right, we see that

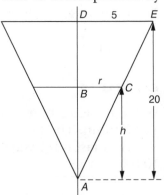

$$\frac{h}{r} = \frac{20}{5}$$

$$20r = 5h$$

$$r = \frac{h}{4}$$

Replacing r in the volume formula, we get V as a function of h:

$$V = \frac{\pi}{3}\left(\frac{h}{4}\right)^2 h$$

$$V = \frac{\pi}{48}h^3$$

Step 4

$$\frac{dV}{dt} = \frac{3\pi}{48}h^2\frac{dh}{dt}$$

$$= \frac{\pi}{16}h^2\frac{dh}{dt}$$

Step 5

$$100 = \frac{\pi}{16}(10)^2\frac{dh}{dt}$$

$$100 = \frac{100\pi}{16} \cdot \frac{dh}{dt}$$

$$1600 = 100\pi\frac{dh}{dt}$$

$$\frac{dh}{dt} = \frac{16}{\pi}$$

The water level is rising at the rate of $\dfrac{16}{\pi}$ ft/min.

Supplementary Problems

1. A spherical snowball is melting in such a way that its surface area decreases at the rate of 1 in²/min.
    (a) How fast is its radius shrinking when it is 3 in?
    (b) How fast is its volume shrinking when its radius is 3 in?
2. Two cars begin a trip from the same point P. If car A travels north at the rate of 30 mi/h and car B travels west at the rate of 40 mi/h, how fast is the distance between them changing 2 hours later?
3. Ship A is 70 km west of ship B and is sailing south at the rate of 25 km/h. Ship B is sailing north at the rate of 45 km/h. How fast is the distance between the two ships changing 2 hours later?

4. A baseball diamond is a square whose sides are 90 ft long. If a batter hits a ball and runs to first base at the rate of 20 ft/sec, how fast is his distance from second base changing when he has run 50 ft?

5. Two legs of a right triangle are each 70 cm. If one leg grows at the rate of 5 cm/min and the other shrinks at the rate of 5 cm/min,
   (a) How fast is the hypotenuse of the triangle changing 2 minutes later?
   (b) How fast is the area of the triangle changing 2 minutes later?

6. A fisherman has a fish at the end of his line, which is being reeled in at the rate of 2 ft/sec from a bridge 30 ft above the water. At what speed is the fish moving through the water toward the bridge when the amount of line out is 50 ft? (Assume the fish is at the surface of the water and there is no sag in the line.)

7. Sand is being dumped from a dump truck at the rate of 10 ft^3/min and forms a pile in the shape of a cone whose height is always half its radius. How fast is its height rising when the pile is 5 ft high?

8. A radar station is 2000 ft from the launch site of a rocket. If the rocket is launched vertically at the rate of 500 ft/sec, how fast is the distance between the radar station and the rocket changing 10 seconds later?

Solutions to Supplementary Problems

1. Let S represent the surface area of the sphere.

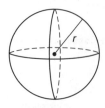

(a) The surface area of a sphere is $S = 4\pi r^2$.

Given: $\dfrac{dS}{dt} = -1$ Find: $\dfrac{dr}{dt}$ when $r = 3$.

$$S = 4\pi r^2$$

$$\frac{dS}{dt} = 8\pi r \frac{dr}{dt}$$

When $r = 3$,

$$-1 = 24\pi \frac{dr}{dt}$$

$$\frac{dr}{dt} = -\frac{1}{24\pi}$$

Because $\dfrac{dr}{dt}$ is negative, r is *shrinking* at the rate of $\dfrac{1}{24\pi}$ in/min.

(b) The volume of a sphere is $V = \dfrac{4}{3}\pi r^3$.

Given: $\dfrac{dS}{dt} = -1$

Find: $\dfrac{dV}{dt}$ when $r = 3$.

$$V = \frac{4}{3}\pi r^3$$

$$\frac{dV}{dt} = 4\pi r^2 \frac{dr}{dt}$$

From part (a), $\dfrac{dr}{dt} = -\dfrac{1}{24\pi}$ when $r = 3$.

$$\frac{dV}{dt} = 4\pi \cdot 3^2 \left(-\frac{1}{24\pi}\right)$$

$$= -\frac{36\pi}{24\pi}$$

$$= -\frac{3}{2}$$

The volume is shrinking at the rate of $1\,{}^1\!/2$ in^3/min.

2.

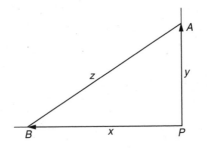

Given: $\dfrac{dx}{dt} = 40$ $\dfrac{dy}{dt} = 30$ Find: $\dfrac{dz}{dt}$ 2 hours later

From the diagram,

$$z^2 = x^2 + y^2$$

$$2z\frac{dz}{dt} = 2x\frac{dx}{dt} + 2y\frac{dy}{dt}$$

$$z\frac{dz}{dt} = x\frac{dx}{dt} + y\frac{dy}{dt}$$

Two hours after the cars leave their initial point, $x = 80$ miles $(2 \times 40 = 80)$ and $y = 60$ miles $(2 \times 30 = 60)$. It follows that

$$z^2 = 80^2 + 60^2$$

$$= 6400 + 3600$$

$$= 10,000$$

$$z = 100$$

Substituting $x = 80$, $y = 60$, $z = 100$, $\dfrac{dx}{dt} = 40$, and $\dfrac{dy}{dt} = 30$, we obtain

$$100\frac{dz}{dt} = 80 \cdot 40 + 60 \cdot 30$$

$$100\frac{dz}{dt} = 5000$$

$$\frac{dz}{dt} = 50$$

The distance between the cars is increasing at the rate of 50 mi/h.

3.

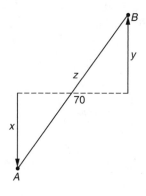

Given: $\dfrac{dx}{dt} = 25$ $\dfrac{dy}{dt} = 45$

Find: $\dfrac{dz}{dt}$ 2 hours later

The relationship between x and y is easily obtained if we look at the diagram just the right way.

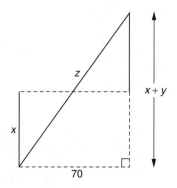

By the theorem of Pythagoras, $z^2 = (x + y)^2 + 70^2$. Differentiating,

$$2z\frac{dz}{dt} = 2(x + y)\left(\frac{dx}{dt} + \frac{dy}{dt}\right) + 0$$

$$z\frac{dz}{dt} = (x + y)\left(\frac{dx}{dt} + \frac{dy}{dt}\right)$$

After 2 hours, $x = 2 \times 25 = 50$ and $y = 2 \times 45 = 90$. It follows that $z^2 = 140^2 + 70^2 = 24{,}500$ and $z = \sqrt{24{,}500} = 70\sqrt{5}$.

$$70\sqrt{5}\frac{dz}{dt} = (50 + 90)(25 + 45)$$

$$70\sqrt{5}\frac{dz}{dt} = 9800$$

$$\frac{dz}{dt} = \frac{9800}{70\sqrt{5}} = \frac{140}{\sqrt{5}} = 28\sqrt{5} \text{ km/h}$$

4.

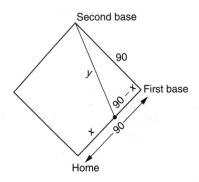

Given: $\dfrac{dx}{dt} = 20$ Find: $\dfrac{dy}{dt}$ when $x = 50$

From the diagram, $90^2 + (90 - x)^2 = y^2$.
Differentiating,

$$0 + 2(90 - x)\left(-\frac{dx}{dt}\right) = 2y\frac{dy}{dt}$$

$$-(90 - x)\frac{dx}{dt} = y\frac{dy}{dt}$$

When $x = 50$,

$$90^2 + (90 - 50)^2 = y^2$$

$$8100 + 1600 = y^2$$

$$y = \sqrt{9700} = 10\sqrt{97}$$

Substituting $x = 50$, $y = 10\sqrt{97}$, and $\dfrac{dx}{dt} = 20$, we obtain

$$(-40)(20) = 10\sqrt{97}\,\frac{dy}{dt}$$

$$\frac{dy}{dt} = -\frac{800}{10\sqrt{97}} = -\frac{80}{\sqrt{97}}$$

The negative sign indicates that the runner's distance to second base is *decreasing* at the rate of $80/\sqrt{97}$ (approximately 8.1) ft/sec.

5.

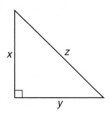

Given: $\dfrac{dx}{dt} = 5$ Find: (a) $\dfrac{dz}{dt}$ 2 minutes later

$\dfrac{dy}{dt} = -5$ (b) $\dfrac{dA}{dt}$ 2 minutes later

(a) $$z^2 = x^2 + y^2$$

$$2z\frac{dz}{dt} = 2x\frac{dx}{dt} + 2y\frac{dy}{dt}$$

$$z\frac{dz}{dt} = x\frac{dx}{dt} + y\frac{dy}{dt}$$

After 2 minutes, $x = 70 + 10 = 80$ cm and $y = 70 - 10 = 60$ cm. At this instant, $z = \sqrt{80^2 + 60^2} = 100$ cm.

$$100\frac{dz}{dt} = 80 \cdot 5 + 60 \cdot (-5)$$

$$= 400 - 300$$

65

$$100\frac{dz}{dt} = 100$$

$$\frac{dz}{dt} = 1$$

The hypotenuse is growing at the rate of 1 cm/min.

(b)
$$A = \frac{1}{2}xy$$

$$\frac{dA}{dt} = \frac{1}{2}\left(x\frac{dy}{dt} + y\frac{dx}{dt}\right)$$

As in part (a) after 2 minutes $x = 80$ cm and $y = 60$ cm.

$$\frac{dA}{dt} = \frac{1}{2}[80 \cdot (-5) + 60 \cdot 5]$$

$$= -50$$

The area is *decreasing* at the rate of 50 cm^2/min.

6.

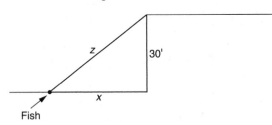

Fish

Given: $\dfrac{dz}{dt} = -2$ Find: $\dfrac{dx}{dt}$ when $z = 50$

From the theorem of Pythagoras,

$$z^2 = x^2 + 30^2$$

Differentiating,

$$2z\frac{dz}{dt} = 2x\frac{dx}{dt} + 0$$

$$z\frac{dz}{dt} = x\frac{dx}{dt}$$

When $z = 50$,

$$50^2 = x^2 + 30^2$$

$$2500 = x^2 + 900$$

$$x^2 = 1600$$

$$x = 40$$

Substituting the appropriate values,

$$50(-2) = 40\frac{dx}{dt}$$

$$\frac{dx}{dt} = \frac{-100}{40} = -\frac{5}{2}$$

The speed of the fish is $2^1/_2$ ft/sec. The negative rate indicates that x is shrinking. (The fish is moving toward the bridge.)

7.

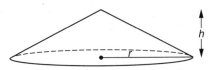

Given: $\dfrac{dV}{dt} = 10$ Find: $\dfrac{dh}{dt}$ when $h = 5$.

The volume of a cone is related to its height and radius by the equation $V = \dfrac{\pi}{3} r^2 h$. Since $h = \dfrac{1}{2} r$, it follows that $r = 2h$, so

$$V = \frac{\pi}{3}(2h)^2 h$$

$$= \frac{4\pi}{3} h^3$$

Differentiating with respect to t,

$$\frac{dV}{dt} = 4\pi h^2 \frac{dh}{dt}$$

Substituting the given information,

$$10 = 4\pi \cdot 5^2 \frac{dh}{dt}$$

$$10 = 100\pi \frac{dh}{dt}$$

$$\frac{dh}{dt} = \frac{1}{10\pi}$$

The height of the cone is rising at the rate of $\frac{1}{10\pi}$ ft/min.

8.

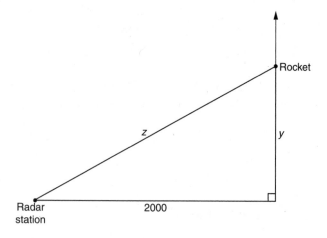

Given: $\dfrac{dy}{dt} = 500$ Find: $\dfrac{dz}{dt}$ 10 seconds later

By the Pythagorean theorem,

$$z^2 = y^2 + 2000^2$$

Differentiating,

$$2z\frac{dz}{dt} = 2y\frac{dy}{dt}$$

$$z\frac{dz}{dt} = y\frac{dy}{dt}$$

10 seconds after the rocket is launched, $y = 10 \times 500 = 5000$ ft.

$$z^2 = 5000^2 + 2000^2$$

$$= 25,000,000 + 4,000,000$$

$$= 29,000,000$$

$$z = 1000\sqrt{29}$$

Substituting,

$$1000\sqrt{29}\frac{dz}{dt} = 5000(500)$$

$$1000\sqrt{29}\frac{dz}{dt} = 2,500,000$$

$$\frac{dz}{dt} = \frac{2500}{\sqrt{29}}$$

The distance between the rocket and the radar station is increasing at the rate of $2500/\sqrt{29}$ (approximately 464.2) ft/sec.

Chapter 4

Applied Maximum and Minimum

Optimization problems are one of the most important applications of differential calculus. Whether we are concerned with how to get from A to B in the least amount of time, or we wish to construct a box of maximum volume for a given amount of material, we are looking for the "best" way to perform a given task.

The problem of optimization generally reduces to the problem of finding the maximum or minimum value of a function subject to a given set of conditions or constraints. In this chapter we will discuss how to set up a maximum/minimum problem and solve it to find the optimal solution.

We begin by reviewing a few basic definitions and theorems.

A function f has an absolute maximum on an interval I if there exists a number c in I such that $f(x) \leq f(c)$ for all x in I.

A similar definition (with the inequality reversed) applies to an absolute minimum. Note that that absolute maximum or minimum value is $f(c)$. Its location is $x = c$.

The existence of an absolute maximum and minimum under certain conditions is guaranteed by the *Extreme Value Theorem*:

> If f is continuous on a closed bounded interval $I = [a, b]$, then f has both an absolute maximum and an absolute minimum in I.

Of course, f *may* have an absolute maximum and/or minimum if the function fails to be continuous or if I is not closed, but there is no *guarantee* of their existence unless both hypotheses of the extreme value theorem are satisfied.

> A critical number for f is a number x for which either $f'(x) = 0$ or $f'(x)$ does not exist.

In a word problem arising from a physical or geometrical situation it is very rare that $f'(x)$ will fail to exist. Therefore, in this book we will consider only critical numbers for which $f'(x) = 0$.

It is easily shown that if a function is continuous on a closed bounded interval, then its absolute extrema (which exist by the Extreme Value Theorem) will occur either at a critical number or at an endpoint of the interval. The following procedure, which we will call the "closed interval method," can be used to determine their values.

> **Step 1**
> Find all critical numbers of $f(x)$ that lie within the given interval $[a, b]$. Critical numbers outside the interval may be ignored.
>
> **Step 2**
> Compute the values of $f(x)$ at each critical number and at the endpoints a and b.
>
> **Step 3**
> The largest value of $f(x)$ obtained in step 2 is the absolute maximum and the smallest value is the absolute minimum.

EXAMPLE I

Find the absolute maximum and minimum value of $f(x) = x^3 - 12x + 5$ on the interval $[-1, 4]$

Solution

Step I

$$f(x) = x^3 - 12x + 5$$
$$f'(x) = 3x^2 - 12$$
$$0 = 3x^2 - 12$$
$$12 = 3x^2$$
$$4 = x^2$$
$$x = 2 \qquad x = -2$$

Step 2

The value $x = -2$ is outside the interval and is therefore ignored.

x	$f(x)$
-1	16
2	-11
4	21

Step 3

The absolute maximum of $f(x)$ on $[-1, 4]$ is 21 and the absolute minimum is -11.

Most functions that occur in connection with maximum/minimum problems will be continuous, but occasionally the interval representing their domain will be open or infinite in length. In such situations, the closed interval method fails. In fact, the function may not even have absolute extrema.

The function $f(x) = x^2$ on the open interval $(-2, 3)$ has an absolute minimum (of 0) at $x = 0$ but has no absolute maximum. Additional examples can easily be constructed where we have a maximum but no minimum, or neither a maximum nor a minimum. The only time we are *guaranteed* to have both is when we have a continuous function on a closed interval.

Closely related to an absolute maximum is a relative (or local) maximum.

A function f has a relative (or local) maximum at c if there exists an open interval I containing c for which $f(x) \leq f(c)$ for all x in I.

Of course, there is a corresponding definition for a relative minimum. The only difference is that the inequality is reversed.

It can be shown that if $f(x)$ has a relative extremum (maximum or minimum) at c, then c must be a critical number of the function. But the converse is *not true*. A function may have a critical value that corresponds to *neither* a maximum nor a minimum.

Consider, for example, $f(x) = x^3$. Since $f'(x) = 3x^2$, and $f'(0) = 0$, 0 is a critical value for f. But 0 is neither a relative maximum nor a relative minimum. A quick look at its graph shows why.

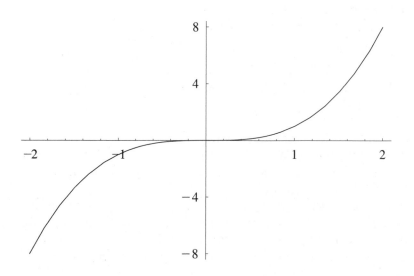

Because it is impossible to find an open interval containing 0 for which (0, 0) is the highest point, f does not have a relative maximum at 0. Similarly, it is impossible to find an open interval containing 0 for which (0, 0) is the lowest point, so f does not have a relative minimum at 0. f has no relative extremum.

To decide whether a critical number is a relative maximum or relative minimum (or perhaps neither) we introduce two tests called the *first derivative test* and the *second derivative test*.

First Derivative Test

Let c be a critical value of f
(a) If $f'(x)$ changes from positive to negative as x goes from the left of c to the right of c, then f has a relative maximum at c.
(b) If $f'(x)$ changes from negative to positive as x goes from the left of c to the right of c, then f has a relative minimum at c.

Second Derivative Test

Let c be a critical value of f
(a) If $f''(c) < 0$, then f has a relative maximum at c.
(b) If $f''(c) > 0$, then f has a relative minimum at c.

If $f''(c) = 0$ the second derivative test fails and the first derivative test must be used. However, this is very rare in solving word problems and the second derivative test is often the more convenient test to use.

When we solve a maximum-minimum problem, we are looking for the largest or smallest value a function can attain. We are looking for the *absolute* maximum or minimum value. Why bother looking for relative extrema? The answer is given in the following theorem:

If a continuous function f has *only one* relative extremum in an interval I at c, then

(a) If the relative extremum is a relative minimum, then f has an absolute minimum at c.

(b) If the relative extremum is a relative maximum, then f has an absolute maximum at c.

Note: If the interval I is closed, this theorem offers a convenient alternative to the closed interval method.

The theorem can be easily understood with the aid of a simple diagram.

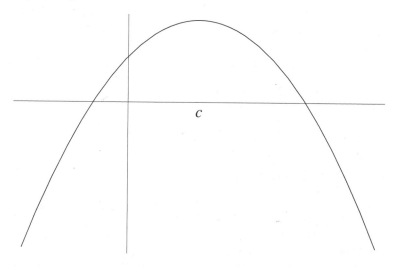

The function shown has a relative maximum at c. Because the function is continuous, the only way this can fail to be the absolute maximum is for the graph to turn around and go higher than $f(c)$. But this would give rise to a relative minimum which, by hypothesis, is impossible. A similar argument holds in the case of a minimum.

Many word problems yield only one relative extremum. To determine whether it is an absolute maximum or minimum, we simply determine whether it is a relative maximum or minimum. This is easily accomplished by using either the first or second derivative tests.

The first step in solving a maximum-minimum word problem is to find a function that represents the quantity to be maximized or minimized. Techniques for accomplishing this task were discussed in Chapter 1 and are summarized below.

Step 1

Draw a diagram (if appropriate). Label all quantities, known and unknown, which are stated in the problem.

Step 2

Write an equation representing the quantity to be maximized or minimized. This quantity will typically be represented in terms of two or more variables.

Step 3

Use any constraints or relationships between the variables to eliminate all but one independent variable. This converts the equation obtained in step 2 into a function. Determine the *domain* of this function appropriate to the problem; i.e., determine the set of all values of the independent variable for which the problem makes sense.

Once the function has been found, we proceed to find its maximum or minimum value.

Step 4

Find all critical numbers.

Step 5

If the function is continuous on a closed interval, use the closed interval method to determine its absolute maximum or minimum values.

OR

If there is *only one* critical value within the interval under consideration, use the first or second derivative test to determine whether it is a relative maximum or relative minimum. The value of the function at this location will be the absolute maximum value or absolute minimum value, respectively.

EXAMPLE 2

Jodi wishes to use 100 feet of fencing to enclose a rectangular garden. Determine the maximum possible area of her garden.

Step 1

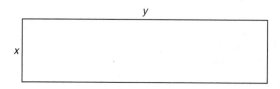

Step 2

$$A = xy$$

Step 3
Since the perimeter of the rectangle is to be 100 feet,

$$2x + 2y = 100$$
$$x + y = 50$$
$$y = 50 - x$$

It follows from step 2 that $A(x) = x(50 - x)$ or $A(x) = 50x - x^2$. Since x cannot be negative, the smallest allowable value of x is 0. Since $y = 50 - x$ and y cannot be negative, the largest allowable value of x is 50.

$$0 \leq x \leq 50$$

Note: In order to obtain a closed interval, we allow $x = 0$ and $x = 50$ as acceptable dimensions. Such *degenerate* rectangles have an area of 0.

Since $A(x) = 50x - x^2$ is a polynomial, its derivative exists everywhere. The critical values occur where $A'(x) = 0$.

$$A(x) = 50x - x^2$$
$$A'(x) = 50 - 2x = 0$$
$$x = 25$$

Step 5
We use the closed interval method.

x	$A(x)$
0	0
25	625
50	0

The maximum area is 625 ft^2.

EXAMPLE 3

What is the minimum possible perimeter for a rectangle whose area is 100 in^2?

Solution

At first glance this problem appears similar to Example 2. We shall see, however, that it is somewhat different and must be solved using another strategy.

Step 1

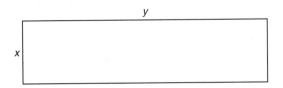

Step 2
We wish to minimize the perimeter.

$$P = 2x + 2y$$

Step 3

The given constraint is that the area must be 100 in^2.

$$xy = 100$$

$$y = \frac{100}{x}$$

Now we can represent P as a function of x

$$P(x) = 2x + 2\left(\frac{100}{x}\right)$$

$$= 2x + \frac{200}{x}$$

$$= 2x + 200x^{-1}$$

At this point the solution takes a different turn. Unlike Example 2, we cannot allow $x = 0$. Not only would this cause difficulty for $P(x)$, but more fundamentally it is *impossible* to have a rectangle with an area of 100 if one side has length 0.

On the other side of the spectrum, what is the largest that x might be? A moment's thought will convince you that no matter how large you make x, you can always take y sufficiently small so that $xy = 100$.

Since the domain of $P(x)$ is the interval $(0, \infty)$ the closed interval method cannot be used here.

Step 4

We find the critical value(s)

$$P'(x) = 2 - 200x^{-2}$$

$$0 = 2 - \frac{200}{x^2}$$

$$\frac{200}{x^2} = 2$$

$$2x^2 = 200$$
$$x^2 = 100$$
$$x = 10$$

> The value $x = -10$ is disregarded since it falls outside the domain of our function ($0 < x < \infty$).

Step 5

We apply the second derivative test to our critical value, $x = 10$.

$$P'(x) = 2 - 200x^{-2} \text{ (from step 4)}$$

$$P''(x) = 400x^{-3} = \frac{400}{x^3}$$

$$P''(10) > 0$$

We do not need to know the exact value of $P''(10)$. The fact that it is positive tells us that we have a relative minimum at $x = 10$. Since $x = 10$ is the only relative extremum, it must be the absolute minimum. Since $y = 100/x$, $y = 10$ when $x = 10$. The minimum perimeter $= 2x + 2y = 40$.

Note: Testing the critical number in a word problem (step 5) may be considered to be an optional step. If you are convinced that the problem has a solution and you find only one critical point, then this point must be the solution to the problem. However, intuition is sometimes misleading, and, from a mathematical perspective, the test is one way to justify the solution.

The next example illustrates the importance of checking the endpoints of the interval.

EXAMPLE 4

A piece of wire 24 inches long is to be used to form a square and/or a rectangle whose length is three times its width. Determine their maximum and minimum *combined* area.

80

Solution

Step 1

Let x be the side of the square and y the width of the rectangle.

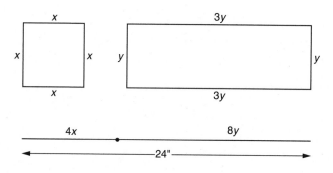

Step 2

$$A = x^2 + 3y^2$$

Step 3

Since the combined perimeter of the two figures must be 24 inches, we have

$$4x + 8y = 24$$

$$x + 2y = 6$$

It follows that $x = 6 - 2y$.

> We can also solve for y. This leads to $y = \dfrac{6 - x}{2}$. In order to avoid fractions, we prefer to solve for x.

Replacing x in terms of y in step 2 gives

$$A(y) = (6 - 2y)^2 + 3y^2$$

Recall that $4x + 8y = 24$. If all of the wire is used to form the square, $y = 0$. If all of the wire is used to form the rectangle, $x = 0$ so $8y = 24$ and $y = 3$. Hence

$$A(y) = (6 - 2y)^2 + 3y^2 \qquad 0 \le y \le 3$$

Step 4

Using the chain rule,

$$A'(y) = 2(6 - 2y)(-2) + 6y$$
$$= -24 + 8y + 6y$$
$$= -24 + 14y$$
$$0 = -24 + 14y$$
$$y = \frac{24}{14} = \frac{12}{7}$$

Step 5

Compute $A(y)$ at the critical numbers and at the endpoints of the interval.

$$A(y) = (6 - 2y)^2 + 3y^2$$
$$A(0) = 36 \qquad \text{← All the wire is used to form the square.}$$
$$A\left(\frac{12}{7}\right) = \left(6 - \frac{24}{7}\right)^2 + 3\left(\frac{12}{7}\right)^2$$
$$= \left(\frac{18}{7}\right)^2 + 3\left(\frac{12}{7}\right)^2$$
$$= \frac{324}{49} + \frac{432}{49}$$
$$= \frac{756}{49} = \frac{108}{7} \approx 15.43$$
$$A(3) = 27 \qquad \text{← All the wire is used to form the rectangle.}$$

The maximum area occurs at the left endpoint of the interval, $y = 0$, when all the wire is used to form the square.

The minimum area occurs when $y = \frac{12}{7}$. To minimize the combined area, the wire should be cut $8y = \frac{96}{7} = 13\frac{5}{7}$ inches from one end and used to form the rectangle. The remaining $10\frac{2}{7}$ inches is used to construct the square.

EXAMPLE 5

An open box is formed by cutting squares of equal size from the corners of a 24 by 15-inch piece of sheet metal and folding up the sides. Determine the size of the cutout that maximizes the volume of the box.

Solution

Step 1

Let x represent the size of the cutout.

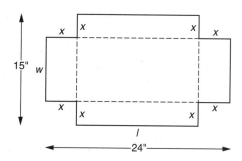

Step 2

$$V = l \times w \times h$$

Step 3

$$l = 24 - 2x$$

$$w = 15 - 2x$$

$$h = x$$

From step 2,

$$V(x) = (24 - 2x)(15 - 2x)(x)$$

$$= 4x^3 - 78x^2 + 360x \qquad 0 \le x \le \frac{15}{2}$$

$$\left(\text{if } x > \frac{15}{2}, w \text{ becomes negative}\right)$$

Step 4

$$V'(x) = 12x^2 - 156x + 360$$
$$0 = 12x^2 - 156x + 360$$
$$0 = 12(x^2 - 13x + 30)$$
$$0 = 12(x - 10)(x - 3)$$
$$x = 10 \qquad x = 3$$

Step 5

The value $x = 10$ may be ignored since it is outside the interval $0 \le x \le \dfrac{15}{2}$.

x	$V(x)$
0	0
3	486
$\dfrac{15}{2}$	0

The maximum volume of 486 in^3 occurs when $x = 3$.

EXAMPLE 6

Find the dimensions of the rectangle of largest area whose base is on the x axis and whose upper two vertices lie on the parabola $y = 12 - x^2$. What is the maximum area?

Solution

Step 1

Let (x, y) be the point on the parabola that meets the corner of the rectangle.

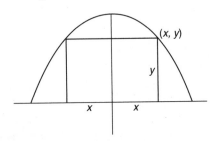

Step 2

The height of the rectangle is y and the width is $2x$. The rectangle's area is $A = 2xy$.

Step 3

Since the upper vertices of the rectangle lie on the parabola, their coordinates must satisfy the equation $y = 12 - x^2$. The area of the rectangle then becomes

$$A(x) = 2x(12 - x^2)$$
$$= 24x - 2x^3 \qquad 0 \le x \le \sqrt{12}$$

Step 4
$$A'(x) = 24 - 6x^2$$
$$0 = 24 - 6x^2$$
$$6x^2 = 24$$
$$x^2 = 4$$
$$x = 2$$

> $x = -2$ lies outside the domain of the function.

Step 5

$A(0) = 0$, $A(2) = 32$, $A(\sqrt{12}) = 0$

If $x = 2$, $y = 12 - x^2 = 8$. Since the width of the rectangle is $2x$, the dimensions of the rectangle are 4×8 and the maximum area is 32.

EXAMPLE 7

A church window is in the shape of a rectangle surmounted by a semicircle. If the perimeter of the window is 20 ft, what is its maximum area?

Solution

Step 1

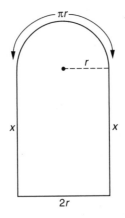

Step 2

The area of the window is the sum of the areas of its rectangular bottom and its semicircular top. Since the area of a whole circle of radius r is πr^2, a semicircle has an area of $\frac{1}{2}\pi r^2$.

$$A = 2rx + \frac{1}{2}\pi r^2$$

Step 3

The window has 4 sides, 3 straight sides and a semicircular top. Since the circumference of a whole circle of radius r is $2\pi r$, the semicircular arc has length πr. Since the perimeter is 20 ft,

$$2x + 2r + \pi r = 20$$

$$x = \frac{20 - 2r - \pi r}{2}$$

We substitute into the equation obtained in step 2 and obtain the area as a function of r.

86

$$A(r) = 2r\left(\frac{20 - 2r - \pi r}{2}\right) + \frac{1}{2}\pi r^2$$

$$= 20r - 2r^2 - \pi r^2 + \frac{1}{2}\pi r^2$$

$$= 20r - 2r^2 - \frac{1}{2}\pi r^2$$

Step 4

$$A(r) = 20r - 2r^2 - \frac{1}{2}\pi r^2$$

$$A'(r) = 20 - 4r - \pi r$$

$$= 20 - (4 + \pi)r$$

$$0 = 20 - (4 + \pi)r$$

$$(4 + \pi)r = 20$$

$$r = \frac{20}{4 + \pi}$$

Step 5 (optional)

$A''(r) = -4 - \pi$. Since $A''(r) < 0$ for all r, it is negative at the critical value. Thus $\dfrac{20}{4 + \pi}$ is a relative maximum. Since it is the only relative extremum, the absolute maximum area occurs at this point.

The maximum area is

$$A\left(\frac{20}{4+\pi}\right) = 20\left(\frac{20}{4+\pi}\right) - 2\left(\frac{20}{4+\pi}\right)^2 - \frac{1}{2}\pi\left(\frac{20}{4+\pi}\right)^2$$

$$= \frac{400}{4+\pi} - \frac{800}{(4+\pi)^2} - \frac{200\pi}{(4+\pi)^2}$$

$$= \frac{400(4+\pi)}{(4+\pi)^2} - \frac{800}{(4+\pi)^2} - \frac{200\pi}{(4+\pi)^2}$$

$$= \frac{1600 + 400\pi - 800 - 200\pi}{(4 + \pi)^2}$$

$$= \frac{800 + 200\pi}{(4 + \pi)^2}$$

$$= \frac{200(4 + \pi)}{(4 + \pi)^2}$$

$$= \frac{200}{4 + \pi} \approx 28.005 \text{ ft}^2$$

EXAMPLE 8

Find the rectangle of largest area that can be inscribed in an equilateral triangle of side 20.

Solution

Step 1

It is convenient to let the width of the rectangle be $2x$. Its height is y.

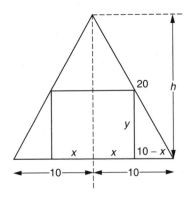

Step 2

The area of the rectangle is $2xy$.

Step 3

By the theorem of Pythagoras, the altitude h of the equilateral triangle can be easily determined:

$$h^2 + 10^2 = 20^2$$
$$h^2 + 100 = 400$$
$$h^2 = 300$$
$$h = \sqrt{300} = 10\sqrt{3}$$

Observing similar triangles, $\dfrac{10 - x}{10} = \dfrac{y}{10\sqrt{3}}$. Multiplying, we get

$$10y = 10\sqrt{3}(10 - x)$$
$$y = \sqrt{3}(10 - x)$$

The area as a function of x may be written

$$A(x) = 2x\sqrt{3}(10 - x)$$
$$= 2\sqrt{3}(10x - x^2)$$

From the diagram it is clear that $0 \leq x \leq 10$

Step 4
$$A'(x) = 2\sqrt{3}(10 - 2x)$$
$$0 = 2\sqrt{3}(10 - 2x)$$
$$0 = 10 - 2x$$
$$2x = 10$$
$$x = 5$$

The corresponding value of $y = \sqrt{3}(10 - x) = 5\sqrt{3}$. Since the dimensions of the rectangle were $2x$ and y, the largest possible area is $10 \times 5\sqrt{3} = 50\sqrt{3}$.

Step 5 (optional)
If $x = 0$ or $x = 10$, the area of the rectangle is 0. Therefore, the absolute maximum area occurs at $x = 5$.

EXAMPLE 9

A river is 1 mile wide. Frank wants to get from point A to point B on the opposite side of the river, 3 miles downstream. If Frank can run 5 miles per hour and can swim 3 miles per hour, what is the least amount of time in which he can get from A to B?

Solution

Step 1

Let C be the point on the other side of the river directly opposite A. Let D be the point between C and B that Frank should swim to; he will run the rest of the way to B. Let x be the distance from C to D.

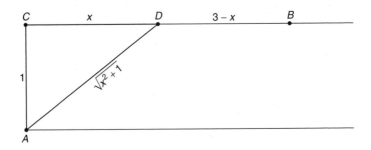

Steps 2 and 3

Since $d = r \times t$, the time necessary to either run or swim is determined by $t = d/r$.

$$t_{\text{swim}} = \frac{d_{\text{swim}}}{r_{\text{swim}}} = \frac{\sqrt{x^2 + 1}}{3}$$

$$t_{\text{run}} = \frac{d_{\text{run}}}{r_{\text{run}}} = \frac{3 - x}{5}$$

The total time to go from A to B is $t_{\text{swim}} + t_{\text{run}}$ so

$t(x) = \dfrac{\sqrt{x^2 + 1}}{3} + \dfrac{3 - x}{5}$. It is clear that $0 \leq x \leq 3$.

Step 4

For ease in differentiation, we rewrite $t(x)$ using exponents:

$$t(x) = \frac{1}{3}(x^2 + 1)^{1/2} + \frac{1}{5}(3 - x)$$

$$t'(x) = \frac{1}{6}(x^2 + 1)^{-1/2}(2x) + \frac{1}{5}(-1)$$

$$= \frac{x}{3\sqrt{x^2 + 1}} - \frac{1}{5}$$

We set the derivative to 0 and solve for x.

$$0 = \frac{x}{3\sqrt{x^2 + 1}} - \frac{1}{5}$$

$$\frac{1}{5} = \frac{x}{3\sqrt{x^2 + 1}}$$

$$5x = 3\sqrt{x^2 + 1}$$

$$25x^2 = 9(x^2 + 1)$$

$$25x^2 = 9x^2 + 9$$

$$16x^2 = 9$$

$$x^2 = \frac{9}{16}$$

$$x = \frac{3}{4}$$

Step 5

Before we jump to any conclusion about the route Frank should take, let us examine the endpoints of the interval.
Recall that $t(x) = \dfrac{\sqrt{x^2 + 1}}{3} + \dfrac{3 - x}{5}$.

$$x = 0 \qquad t(0) = \frac{1}{3} + \frac{3}{5}$$

$$= \frac{14}{15} \text{ h (56 minutes)}$$

$$x = \frac{3}{4} \qquad t\left(\frac{3}{4}\right) = \frac{\sqrt{\left(\frac{3}{4}\right)^2 + 1}}{3} + \frac{3 - \frac{3}{4}}{5}$$

$$= \frac{\sqrt{\frac{9}{16} + 1}}{3} + \frac{\frac{9}{4}}{5} = \frac{\frac{5}{4}}{3} + \frac{\frac{9}{4}}{5}$$

$$= \frac{5}{12} + \frac{9}{20} = \frac{208}{240}$$

$$= \frac{13}{15} \text{ h (52 minutes)}$$

$$x = 3 \qquad t(3) = \frac{\sqrt{10}}{3} \approx 1.054 \text{ h (63.2 minutes)}$$

The minimum time to go from A to B is $\dfrac{13}{15}$ h.

EXAMPLE 10

What is the largest possible volume a right circular cylinder can have if it is inscribed in a sphere of radius 5?

Solution

Step 1

We examine the figure geometrically from a two-dimensional perspective.

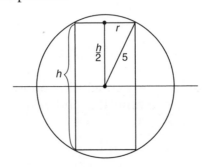

92

Step 2

The volume of a right circular cylinder of radius r and height h is $V = \pi r^2 h$.

Step 3

If we draw a radius to the point where the sphere and cylinder meet, we see from the theorem of Pythagoras that

$$r^2 + \left(\frac{h}{2}\right)^2 = 5^2$$

$$r^2 + \frac{h^2}{4} = 25$$

$$r^2 = 25 - \frac{h^2}{4}$$

> Since the volume equation requires r^2, it is more convenient to solve for r in terms of h. Although solving for h in terms of r would also work, an extra radical is introduced, which makes the calculus more difficult.

Substituting into the volume equation obtained in step 2,

$$V(h) = \pi \left(25 - \frac{h^2}{4}\right)h \qquad 0 \le h \le 10$$

$$= \pi \left(25h - \frac{1}{4}h^3\right)$$

Step 4

$$V'(h) = \pi \left(25 - \frac{3}{4}h^2\right)$$

$$0 = \pi \left(25 - \frac{3}{4}h^2\right)$$

$$0 = 25 - \frac{3}{4}h^2$$

$$\frac{3}{4}h^2 = 25$$

$$h^2 = \frac{100}{3}$$

$$h = \frac{10}{\sqrt{3}}$$

Step 5 (optional)

Since $V(0) = 0$ and $V(10) = 0$, the maximum volume must occur when $h = \dfrac{10}{\sqrt{3}}$. The corresponding value of r may be computed from the equation $r^2 = 25 - \dfrac{h^2}{4}$

$$r^2 = 25 - \dfrac{\dfrac{100}{3}}{4}$$

$$= 25 - \dfrac{25}{3}$$

$$= \dfrac{50}{3}$$

$$r = \dfrac{\sqrt{50}}{\sqrt{3}} = \dfrac{5\sqrt{2}}{\sqrt{3}} = \dfrac{5}{3}\sqrt{6}$$

The maximum volume is $\pi r^2 h = \pi \left(\dfrac{50}{3}\right)\left(\dfrac{10}{\sqrt{3}}\right) = \dfrac{500\pi}{3\sqrt{3}}$.

EXAMPLE 11

A closed rectangular box with a square base is to have a surface area of 150 in². What is the maximum possible volume such a box can contain?

Solution

Step 1

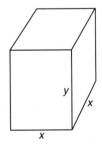

Step 2

The volume of a box is length × width × height. According to the diagram, $V = x^2 y$.

Step 3

The surface area of the box is the sum of the areas of its six sides. The top and bottom each have an area of x^2 and each of the four sides of the box has an area of xy.

$$2x^2 + 4xy = 150$$

$$x^2 + 2xy = 75$$

$$y = \frac{75 - x^2}{2x}$$

$$V(x) = x^2 \left(\frac{75 - x^2}{2x} \right)$$

$$= \frac{x}{2}(75 - x^2)$$

$$= \frac{1}{2}(75x - x^3)$$

Step 4

$$V'(x) = \frac{1}{2}(75 - 3x^2)$$

$$0 = \frac{1}{2}(75 - 3x^2)$$

$$0 = 75 - 3x^2$$

$$3x^2 = 75$$

$$x^2 = 25$$

$$x = 5$$

$y = \dfrac{75 - x^2}{2x} = \dfrac{75 - 25}{10} = \dfrac{50}{10} = 5;$ the corresponding volume $= x^2 y = 125$ in³.

Step 5 (Optional. If you are convinced that the box must have a maximum volume, stop here.)

$$V''(x) = -3x \qquad V''(5) < 0$$

V has a relative maximum at 5. Since it is the only relative extremum for positive x, the absolute maximum volume is 125 in^3.

EXAMPLE 12

A cylindrical can is to contain 2000 in^3 of liquid. What dimensions will minimize the amount of metal used in the construction of the can?

Solution

Step 1
Let r and h represent the radius and height, respectively, of the can.

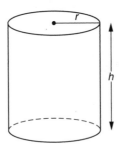

Step 2
$$S = 2\pi r h + 2\pi r^2$$

Step 3
Since the volume of the can must be 2000 in^3,

$$\pi r^2 h = 2000$$

$$h = \frac{2000}{\pi r^2}$$

Substituting into the equation for S obtained in step 2, we obtain S as a function of r.

$$S(r) = 2\pi r \left(\frac{2000}{\pi r^2} \right) + 2\pi r^2$$

$$S(r) = \frac{4000}{r} + 2\pi r^2 \qquad 0 < r < \infty$$

Step 4

$$S(r) = 4000r^{-1} + 2\pi r^2$$

$$S'(r) = -4000r^{-2} + 4\pi r$$

$$0 = -\frac{4000}{r^2} + 4\pi r$$

$$\frac{4000}{r^2} = 4\pi r$$

$$4\pi r^3 = 4000$$

$$r^3 = \frac{1000}{\pi}$$

$$r = \frac{10}{\sqrt[3]{\pi}} \text{ in}$$

Since $h = \dfrac{2000}{\pi r^2}$, the corresponding height is

$$h = \frac{2000}{\pi \left(\dfrac{10}{\sqrt[3]{\pi}} \right)^2} = \frac{2000}{\pi \left(\dfrac{100}{\pi^{2/3}} \right)} = \frac{2000}{100\pi^{1/3}} = \frac{20}{\sqrt[3]{\pi}} \text{ in}$$

Step 5

$$S''(r) = 8000r^{-3} + 4\pi$$

$$= \frac{8000}{r^3} + 4\pi$$

It is clear, even without precise calculation, that since the critical value is positive, S'' will be positive at $10/\sqrt[3]{\pi}$. Therefore, this solution yields a relative minimum surface area. Being the only relative extremum on the interval $(0, \infty)$, $S(r)$ has an absolute minimum at this location.

EXAMPLE 13

Find the point on the line $3x + y = 6$ closest to $(2, 3)$.

Solution

Step 1
Let (x, y) be a point on the line.

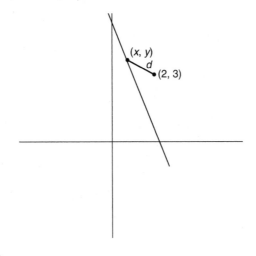

Step 2
The distance between (x, y) and $(2, 3)$ is

$$d = \sqrt{(x - 2)^2 + (y - 3)^2}$$

$$= \sqrt{x^2 + y^2 - 4x - 6y + 13}$$

> The distance between (x_1, y_1) and (x_2, y_2) is
> $$d = \sqrt{(x_2 - x_1)^2 + (y_2 - y_1)^2}$$

Step 3
Since the point (x, y) lies on the line, $y = 6 - 3x$,

$$d = \sqrt{x^2 + (6 - 3x)^2 - 4x - 6(6 - 3x) + 13}$$

Step 4

Differentiating this expression is a little messy due to the presence of the radical. There is a simple trick that can be used to make the calculation easier. Instead of minimizing d, we minimize d^2. Since the value of d^2 is smallest when d is smallest, minimizing d^2 will lead to the same point that minimizes d.

For convenience, let $D = d^2$.

$$D(x) = x^2 + (6 - 3x)^2 - 4x - 6(6 - 3x) + 13$$

$$= x^2 + 36 - 36x + 9x^2 - 4x - 36 + 18x + 13$$

$$= 10x^2 - 22x + 13$$

$$D'(x) = 20x - 22$$

$$0 = 20x - 22$$

$$x = \frac{11}{10} \qquad y = 6 - 3x = \frac{60}{10} - \frac{33}{10} = \frac{27}{10}$$

A glance at the figure should convince you that a minimum distance certainly exists. Since $x = \dfrac{11}{10}$ is the only critical number, the point $\left(\dfrac{11}{10}, \dfrac{27}{10}\right)$ is the point on the line closest to (2, 3).

EXAMPLE 14

A rectangular poster, which is to contain 50 in^2 of print, must have margins of 2 in on each side and 4 in on the top and bottom. What dimensions will minimize the amount of material used?

Solution

Step 1

Although we could let x and y represent the dimensions of the poster, it turns out that labeling the inner rectangle containing the print leads to a simpler solution.

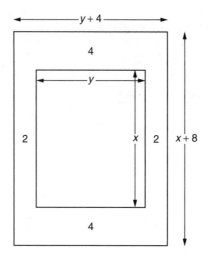

Step 2
We wish to minimize the *outer* rectangular area of the poster.

$$A = (x + 8)(y + 4)$$

$$= xy + 8y + 4x + 32$$

Step 3
Since the inner rectangle must have an area of 50 in^2

$$xy = 50$$

$$y = \frac{50}{x}$$

The area to be minimized may be expressed as a function of x.

$$A(x) = 50 + 8\left(\frac{50}{x}\right) + 4x + 32 \qquad 0 < x < \infty$$

$$= 82 + 400x^{-1} + 4x$$

Step 4

$$A'(x) = -400x^{-2} + 4$$

$$0 = -\frac{400}{x^2} + 4$$

$$\frac{400}{x^2} = 4$$

$$4x^2 = 400$$

$$x^2 = 100$$

$$x = 10$$

Since $y = 50/x$, the corresponding value of y is 5. The dimensions of the poster are $x + 8 = 18$ in by $y + 4 = 9$ in.

Step 5 (Optional)

$$A'(x) = -400x^{-2} + 4$$

$$A''(x) = 800x^{-3}$$

$$= \frac{800}{x^3}$$

$$A''(10) = \frac{800}{1000} > 0$$

A positive second derivative at the critical number tells us we have a relative minimum. Because there is only one relative extremum on the interval $(0, \infty)$, $A(x)$ has an absolute minimum at 10.

EXAMPLE 15

At 12:00 noon ship B is 100 miles east of ship A. If ship B sails west at 10 mi/h and ship A sails south at 20 mi/h, when will the ships be closest to each other? What is the distance between them at that time?

Solution

Step 1

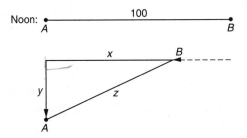

Step 2

The distance between the ships is determined by the theorem of Pythagoras:

$$z = \sqrt{x^2 + y^2}$$

Step 3

Since ship B is traveling 10 mi/h, after t hours $x = 100 - 10t$. Similarly, $y = 20t$. Thus

$$z = \sqrt{(100 - 10t)^2 + (20t)^2}$$
$$= \sqrt{10{,}000 - 2000t + 100t^2 + 400t^2}$$
$$= \sqrt{500t^2 - 2000t + 10{,}000}$$

Step 4

Because of the radical, it is more convenient to minimize z^2 rather than z. The value of t that minimizes z^2 is the same value that minimizes z.

$$\text{Let } F(t) = 500t^2 - 2000t + 10{,}000$$
$$F'(t) = 1000t - 2000$$
$$0 = 1000t - 2000$$
$$t = 2$$

Intuitively it is obvious that there is some point in time when the ships are closest. Since $t = 2$ is the only critical number, the ships must be closest at 2:00 and the minimum distance between them is $z = \sqrt{500(2)^2 - 2000(2) + 10{,}000} = \sqrt{8000} = 40\sqrt{5}$ miles. We can use the second derivative test to confirm this mathematically.

Step 5 (optional)

Since $F''(t) = 1000 > 0$, $t = 2$ yields a relative minimum. Since it is the only relative extremum, it is the absolute minimum.

102

EXAMPLE 16

A conical cup is constructed from a circular piece of paper of radius 5 in by cutting out a sector and joining the resulting edges. What is the maximum volume of the cup?

Solution

Step 1

Join AB to AC

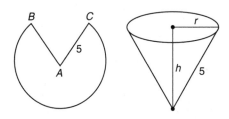

Step 2

The volume of the resulting cone is $V = \dfrac{\pi}{3}r^2h.$

Step 3

From the diagram in step 1 it is apparent that $h^2 + r^2 = 25$. It follows that $r^2 = 25 - h^2$.

$$V = \frac{\pi}{3}r^2h$$

$$= \frac{\pi}{3}(25 - h^2)h$$

$$V(h) = \frac{\pi}{3}(25h - h^3) \qquad 0 \le h \le 5$$

Step 4

$$V'(h) = \frac{\pi}{3}(25 - 3h^2)$$

$$0 = \frac{\pi}{3}(25 - 3h^2)$$

$$0 = 25 - 3h^2$$

$$3h^2 = 25$$

103

$$h^2 = \frac{25}{3}$$

$$h = \frac{5}{\sqrt{3}}$$

The corresponding value of r is $\sqrt{\dfrac{50}{3}}$ inches ($r = \sqrt{25 - h^2}$) and the maximum volume is

$$\frac{\pi}{3}r^2 h = \frac{\pi}{3}\left(\frac{50}{3}\right)\left(\frac{5}{\sqrt{3}}\right)$$

$$= \frac{250\pi}{9\sqrt{3}} \text{ in}^3$$

Step 5 (Optional)

$$V''(h) = \frac{\pi}{3}(-6h) = -2\pi h$$

$$V''\left(\frac{5}{\sqrt{3}}\right) = -\frac{10\pi}{\sqrt{3}} < 0$$

By the second derivative test V has a relative maximum at $h = 5/\sqrt{3}$. Since this is the only relative extremum, it is the location of the absolute maximum.

Supplementary Problems

1. An open field is bounded by a lake with a straight shoreline. A rectangular enclosure is to be constructed using 500 ft of fencing along three sides and the lake as a natural boundary on the fourth side. What dimensions will maximize the enclosed area? What is the maximum area?

2. Ryan has 800 ft of fencing. He wishes to form a rectangular enclosure and then divide it into three sections by running two lengths of fence parallel to one side. What should the dimensions of the enclosure be in order to maximize the enclosed area?

3. 20 meters of fencing are to be laid out in the shape of a right triangle. What should its dimensions be in order to maximize the enclosed area?

4. A piece of wire 100 inches long is to be used to form a square and/or a circle. Determine their (a) maximum and (b) minimum combined area.

5. Find the maximum area of a rectangle inscribed in a semicircle of radius 5 inches if its base lies along the diameter of the semicircle.

6. An open box is to be constructed from a 12- × 12-inch piece of cardboard by cutting away squares of equal size from the four corners and folding up the sides. Determine the size of the cutout that maximizes the volume of the box.

7. A window is to be constructed in the shape of an equilateral triangle on top of a rectangle. If its perimeter is to be 600 cm, what is the maximum possible area of the window?

8. Postal regulations require that the sum of the length and girth of a rectangular package may not exceed 108 inches (the girth is the perimeter of an end of the box). What is the maximum volume of a package with square ends that meets this criteria?

9. A rectangle is inscribed in a right triangle whose sides are 5, 12, and 13 inches. Two adjacent sides of the rectangle lie along the legs of the triangle. What are the dimensions of the rectangle of maximum area? What is the maximum area?

10. Find the dimensions of the right circular cylinder of maximum volume that can be inscribed in a right circular cone whose radius is 3 in and whose height is 10 in. What is the maximum volume?

11. What is the minimum amount of fencing needed to construct a rectangular enclosure containing 1800 ft^2 using a river as a natural boundary on one side?

12. An open rectangular box is to have a base twice as long as it is wide. If its volume must be 972 cm^3, what dimensions will minimize the amount of material used in its construction?

13. Find the points on the parabola $y = x^2$ closest to the point (0, 1).

14. A publisher wants to print a book whose pages are each to have an area of 96 in^2. The margins are to be 1 in on each of three sides and 2 in on the fourth side to allow room for binding. What dimensions will allow the maximum area for the printed region?

15. A closed cylindrical can must have a volume of 1000 in^3. What dimensions will minimize its surface area?

16. A closed cylindrical can must have a volume of 1000 in^3. Its lateral surface is to be constructed from a rectangular piece of metal and its top and bottom are to be stamped from square pieces of metal and the rest of the square discarded. What dimensions will minimize the amount of metal needed in the construction of the can?

17. A rectangle is to be inscribed in the ellipse $\dfrac{x^2}{200} + \dfrac{y^2}{50} = 1$. Determine its maximum possible area.

Solutions to Supplementary Problems

1. The dimensions of the enclosure are labeled x and y as shown.

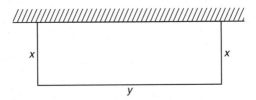

Even though fencing is used on only three sides, the area is still the product of the length and width of the enclosure.

$$A = xy$$

The constraint, however, involves only three sides of the rectangle.

$$2x + y = 500$$

$$y = 500 - 2x$$

Substituting this expression into the area equation, we obtain

$$A(x) = x(500 - 2x)$$

$$= 500x - 2x^2$$

Since x cannot be negative, $x \geq 0$. Since y cannot be negative, $x \leq 250$. (Remember, $y = 500 - 2x$.) The domain of $A(x)$ is the interval $0 \leq x \leq 250$.

Next we determine the critical values of the function $A(x)$.

$$A'(x) = 500 - 4x$$

$$0 = 500 - 4x$$

$$4x = 500$$

$$x = 125 \text{ ft}$$

The maximum area occurs either at the critical value or at an endpoint of the interval. Since $A(0) = 0$ and $A(250) = 0$, the maximum area occurs when $x = 125$. The corresponding value of y is $500 - 2x = 500 - 250 = 250$ ft. The maximum area

$$A_{max} = xy = 125 \times 250 = 31,250 \text{ ft}^2$$

2. Let x and y represent the width and length, respectively, of the enclosure. We will let the interior sections of fence run parallel to the width. (The problem can also be solved by letting the interior pieces run parallel to the length.)

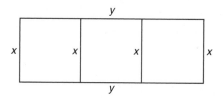

The area of the enclosure is still the product of its length and width.

$$A = xy$$

The 800 ft of fencing is to be divided into six pieces, 4 of length x, and 2 of length y.

$$4x + 2y = 800$$
$$2y = 800 - 4x$$
$$y = 400 - 2x$$

Replacing y by $400 - 2x$ in the area equation, $A = xy$, we obtain the area function

$$A(x) = x(400 - 2x)$$
$$= 400x - 2x^2 \qquad 0 \le x \le 200$$

If $x > 200$, $y < 0$.

The critical values of $A(x)$ are determined by solving $A'(x) = 0$.

$$A'(x) = 400 - 4x$$
$$0 = 400 - 4x$$
$$4x = 400$$
$$x = 100 \text{ ft}$$

Since $A(x)$ is zero at each endpoint of the interval $[0, 200]$, the absolute maximum area occurs at $x = 100$. The corresponding value of y is $400 - 2x = 400 - 200 = 200$ ft. The maximum area $xy = 20,000$ ft^2.

3. Label the legs of the triangle x and y and the hypotenuse z.

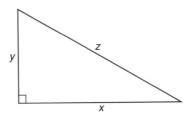

The area of the right triangle is $A = \dfrac{1}{2}xy$. There are two relationships between x, y, and z: $x + y + z = 20$ and $z = \sqrt{x^2 + y^2}$. These may be combined to eliminate z.

$$x + y + \sqrt{x^2 + y^2} = 20$$

We begin by simplifying this equation. To solve for y, we rewrite the equation leaving only the radical on one side.

$$\sqrt{x^2 + y^2} = 20 - (x + y)$$

To eliminate the radical, square both sides of the equation. Then simplify.

$$x^2 + y^2 = 400 - 40(x + y) + (x + y)^2$$
$$x^2 + y^2 = 400 - 40x - 40y + x^2 + 2xy + y^2$$
$$0 = 400 - 40x - 40y + 2xy$$

To solve for y in terms of x, we bring all terms involving y to the left side of the equation. Terms not involving y remain on the right.

$$40y - 2xy = 400 - 40x$$

$$20y - xy = 200 - 20x$$

Finally we factor y from each term on the left and divide by its coefficient.

$$(20 - x)y = 200 - 20x$$

$$y = \frac{200 - 20x}{20 - x}$$

The smallest allowable value of x, leading to a degenerate triangle, is $x = 0$; the largest value occurs when $y = 0$. Since $x + y + \sqrt{x^2 + y^2} = 20$, when $y = 0$, $2x = 20$ or $x = 10$. Hence $0 \leq x \leq 10$.

To compute the critical values, we first express the area in terms of x.

$$A = \frac{1}{2}xy$$

$$= \frac{1}{2}x\left(\frac{200 - 20x}{20 - x}\right)$$

$$A(x) = \frac{100x - 10x^2}{20 - x}$$

The derivative is calculated using the quotient rule. Once obtained, we set it to 0.

$$A'(x) = \frac{(20 - x)(100 - 20x) - (100x - 10x^2)(-1)}{(20 - x)^2}$$

$$= \frac{2000 - 500x + 20x^2 + 100x - 10x^2}{(20 - x)^2}$$

$$= \frac{10x^2 - 400x + 2000}{(20 - x)^2}$$

$$0 = \frac{10x^2 - 400x + 2000}{(20 - x)^2}$$

$$0 = 10x^2 - 400x + 2000$$

$$0 = x^2 - 40x + 200$$

To find x, we use the quadratic formula: $x = \dfrac{-b \pm \sqrt{b^2 - 4ac}}{2a}$.

$$x = \frac{40 \pm \sqrt{(-40)^2 - 4(1)(200)}}{2}$$

$$= \frac{40 \pm \sqrt{800}}{2}$$

$$= 20 \pm 10\sqrt{2}$$

The value $x = 20 + 10\sqrt{2}$ lies outside the interval $[0, 10]$. Since the triangle's area is 0 at the endpoints of the interval, ($x = 0$ and $x = 10$), $x = 20 - 10\sqrt{2}$ must correspond to the absolute maximum area.

The corresponding value of y is computed from

$$y = \frac{200 - 20x}{20 - x}$$

$$= \frac{200 - 20(20 - 10\sqrt{2})}{20 - (20 - 10\sqrt{2})}$$

$$= \frac{200\sqrt{2} - 200}{10\sqrt{2}}$$

$$= \frac{20\sqrt{2} - 20}{\sqrt{2}} \cdot \frac{\sqrt{2}}{\sqrt{2}}$$

$$= \frac{40 - 20\sqrt{2}}{2}$$

$$= 20 - 10\sqrt{2}$$

Since $y = x$, the triangle is an isosceles right triangle. The hypotenuse

$$z = x\sqrt{2} = (20 - 10\sqrt{2})\sqrt{2} = 20\sqrt{2} - 20$$

4. Let x be the side of the square and r the radius of the circle.

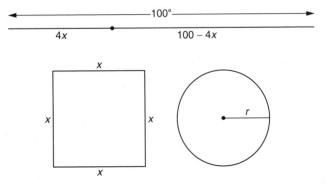

The combined area $A = x^2 + \pi r^2$. Since the combined perimeter of the two figures is equal to the length of the wire,

$$4x + 2\pi r = 100$$

$$2x + \pi r = 50$$

$$r = \frac{50 - 2x}{\pi}$$

Substituting into the area equation,

$$A(x) = x^2 + \pi \left(\frac{50 - 2x}{\pi} \right)^2$$

$$= x^2 + \frac{1}{\pi}(50 - 2x)^2$$

The smallest allowable value of x is 0, in which case all the wire will be used to form the circle. The largest value is $x = 25$, in which case all the wire is used for the square. Hence $0 \leq x \leq 25$.

We take the derivative and compute the critical value.

$$A'(x) = 2x + \frac{2}{\pi}(50 - 2x)(-2)$$

$$= 2x - \frac{4}{\pi}(50 - 2x)$$

$$0 = 2x - \frac{200}{\pi} + \frac{8}{\pi}x$$

$$0 = 2\pi x - 200 + 8x \qquad \leftarrow \text{Multiply by } \pi \text{ to eliminate fractions}$$

$$200 = 2\pi x + 8x$$

$$100 = (\pi + 4)x$$

$$x = \frac{100}{\pi + 4}$$

$A(x) = x^2 + \frac{1}{\pi}(50 - 2x)^2$. Checking the values at the endpoints and critical value,

$$x = 0 \qquad A(0) = \frac{2500}{\pi} \approx 795.78 \qquad \leftarrow \text{Absolute maximum}$$

111

$$x = \frac{100}{\pi + 4} \qquad A\left(\frac{100}{\pi + 4}\right) = \left(\frac{100}{\pi + 4}\right)^2 + \frac{1}{\pi}\left(50 - \frac{200}{\pi + 4}\right)^2$$

$$= \left(\frac{100}{\pi + 4}\right)^2 + \frac{1}{\pi}\left(\frac{50(\pi + 4) - 200}{\pi + 4}\right)^2$$

$$= \left(\frac{100}{\pi + 4}\right)^2 + \frac{1}{\pi}\left(\frac{50\pi}{\pi + 4}\right)^2$$

$$= \frac{10{,}000}{(\pi + 4)^2} + \frac{1}{\pi} \cdot \frac{2500\pi^2}{(\pi + 4)^2}$$

$$= \frac{10{,}000 + 2500\pi}{(\pi + 4)^2}$$

$$= \frac{2500(4 + \pi)}{(\pi + 4)^2}$$

$$= \frac{2500}{\pi + 4} \approx 350.06 \qquad \leftarrow \text{Absolute maximum}$$

$$x = 25 \qquad A(25) = 625$$

Summary: (a) To maximize the combined area, use all the wire to form the circle. (b) To minimize the area, cut the wire at a distance $\dfrac{400}{\pi + 4}$ from one end and form a square. (Remember, the perimeter of the square is $4x$.) The remaining piece of wire is used to form a circle.

5.

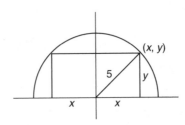

We want to maximize the area of the rectangle. Since its dimensions are $2x$ and y,

$$A = 2xy$$

The point (x, y) lies on the circle so its coordinates must satisfy the equation of the circle. Solving for y,

$$x^2 + y^2 = 25$$
$$y^2 = 25 - x^2$$
$$y = \sqrt{25 - x^2}$$

The area can now be expressed as a function of x. From the diagram it is clear that $0 \leq x \leq 5$.

$$A(x) = 2x\sqrt{25 - x^2}$$
$$= 2x(25 - x^2)^{1/2}$$
$$A'(x) = 2x \cdot \frac{1}{2}(25 - x^2)^{-1/2}(-2x) + 2(25 - x^2)^{1/2}$$
$$0 = \frac{-2x^2}{\sqrt{25 - x^2}} + 2\sqrt{25 - x^2}$$
$$\frac{2x^2}{\sqrt{25 - x^2}} = 2\sqrt{25 - x^2}$$
$$2x^2 = 2(25 - x^2)$$
$$x^2 = 25 - x^2$$
$$2x^2 = 25$$
$$x^2 = \frac{25}{2}$$
$$x = \frac{5}{\sqrt{2}}$$

Since $A(0) = A(5) = 0$, the maximum area is
$$A\left(\frac{5}{\sqrt{2}}\right) = \frac{10}{\sqrt{2}}\sqrt{25 - \frac{25}{2}} = \frac{10}{\sqrt{2}}\sqrt{\frac{25}{2}} = 25 \text{ square inches.}$$

6. Let x represent the side of the square cutout.

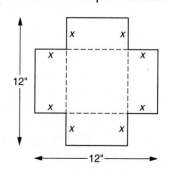

The volume of the box is $V = lwh$ where $l = 12 - 2x$, $w = 12 - 2x$, and $h = x$. Substituting,

$$V(x) = (12 - 2x)^2 x$$
$$= (144 - 48x + 4x^2)x$$
$$= 144x - 48x^2 + 4x^3$$

Since the size of the cutout cannot be negative and cannot exceed 6 inches (otherwise we would cut away more than we have), $0 \le x \le 6$. We next compute the critical values.

$$V'(x) = 144 - 96x + 12x^2$$
$$0 = 144 - 96x + 12x^2$$
$$0 = 12 - 8x + x^2$$
$$0 = (x - 2)(x - 6)$$
$$x = 6 \qquad x = 2$$

If $x = 0$ or $x = 6$, $V(x) = 0$. The maximum volume occurs, therefore, when $x = 2$. The length and width of the box are each $12 - 2x = 8$ inches and the height is 2 inches. The maximum volume is 128 in^3.

7.

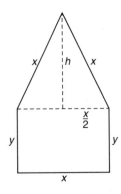

The area of the window is the sum of areas of the rectangular bottom and the triangular top. The area of the rectangle is xy and the area of the triangle is $\dfrac{\sqrt{3}}{4}x^2$. The combined area of the rectangle and triangle is then

$$A = xy + \frac{\sqrt{3}}{4}x^2$$

Since the perimeter of the window is 600 cm,

$$3x + 2y = 600$$
$$2y = 600 - 3x$$
$$y = 300 - \frac{3}{2}x$$

By the theorem of Pythagoras,
$h^2 + \left(\frac{x}{2}\right)^2 = x^2$; it follows that
$h^2 = x^2 - \frac{x^2}{4} = \frac{3}{4}x^2$ and $h = \frac{\sqrt{3}}{2}x$. The area of the equilateral triangle $= \frac{1}{2}xh = \frac{\sqrt{3}}{4}x^2$.

The minimum value of x is 0 and the maximum value, which occurs when $y = 0$, is 200. Hence $0 \le x \le 200$.

$$A(x) = x\left(300 - \frac{3}{2}x\right) + \frac{\sqrt{3}}{4}x^2$$
$$= 300x - \frac{3}{2}x^2 + \frac{\sqrt{3}}{4}x^2$$

Differentiating and setting the derivative equal to 0, we obtain

$$A'(x) = 300 - 3x + \frac{\sqrt{3}}{2}x$$

$$0 = 300 - 3x + \frac{\sqrt{3}}{2}x$$

$$3x - \frac{\sqrt{3}}{2}x = 300$$

$$6x - x\sqrt{3} = 600$$

$$(6 - \sqrt{3})x = 600$$

$$x = \frac{600}{6 - \sqrt{3}}$$

$$A\left(\frac{600}{6 - \sqrt{3}}\right) = 300\left(\frac{600}{6 - \sqrt{3}}\right) - \frac{3}{2}\left(\frac{600}{6 - \sqrt{3}}\right)^2 + \frac{\sqrt{3}}{4}\left(\frac{600}{6 - \sqrt{3}}\right)^2$$
$$= \frac{90,000}{6 - \sqrt{3}} \quad \text{(verify)}$$
$$\approx 21,087 \text{ cm}^2$$

(optional) Since $A''(x) = -3 + \frac{\sqrt{3}}{2} < 0$, $x = \frac{600}{6 - \sqrt{3}}$ yields a

115

relative maximum. Since it is the only relative extremum on $(0, \infty)$, it gives the absolute maximum area.

8.

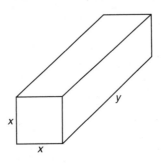

$V = x^2 y$. The postal restrictions say that $4x + y$ cannot exceed 108 inches. For maximum volume we take $4x + y = 108$. Equivalently, $y = 108 - 4x$ and $0 \leq x \leq 27$. (If $x > 27$, $y < 0$.)

$$V(x) = x^2(108 - 4x)$$
$$= 108x^2 - 4x^3$$
$$V'(x) = 216x - 12x^2$$
$$0 = 216x - 12x^2$$
$$0 = 12x(18 - x)$$

The critical values are $x = 0$ and $x = 18$. Since the endpoints of the interval, $x = 0$ and $x = 27$, both yield a volume of 0, the maximum volume occurs when $x = 18$ and its value is

$$V_{max} = V(18) = 18^2(108 - 4 \cdot 18) = 324 \cdot 36 = 11{,}664 \text{ in}^3$$

9.

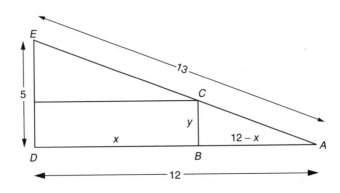

$A = xy$.

Since $\triangle ABC$ is similar to $\triangle ADE$, $\dfrac{y}{5} = \dfrac{12 - x}{12}$. It follows that

$y = \dfrac{5}{12}(12 - x)$, $0 \le x \le 12$. (If $x > 12$, $y < 0$.)

The area, as a function of x, becomes

$$A(x) = x \cdot \frac{5}{12}(12 - x)$$

$$= \frac{5}{12}(12x - x^2)$$

Differentiating, we obtain

$$A'(x) = \frac{5}{12}(12 - 2x)$$

$$0 = \frac{5}{12}(12 - 2x)$$

$$x = 6$$

Since $A(0) = A(12) = 0$, the maximum area occurs when $x = 6$ and $y = \dfrac{5}{12}(12 - 6) = \dfrac{5}{2}$. The maximum area $= xy = 6 \cdot \dfrac{5}{2} = 15$ in^2.

10.

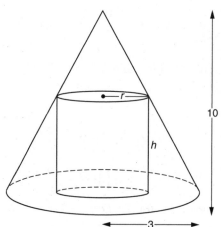

The volume of a cylinder is $V = \pi r^2 h$. To obtain a relationship between r and h, we examine the figure from a two-dimensional perspective.

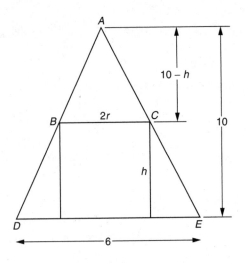

$\triangle ABC$ is similar to $\triangle ADE$. Therefore, their sides are proportional.

$$\frac{2r}{6} = \frac{10 - h}{10}$$

$$20r = 60 - 6h$$

$$6h = 60 - 20r$$

$$h = 10 - \frac{10}{3}r \qquad 0 \le r \le 3$$

By substitution the volume as a function of r is

$$V = \pi r^2 h$$

$$V(r) = \pi r^2 \left(10 - \frac{10}{3}r\right)$$

$$= \pi \left(10r^2 - \frac{10}{3}r^3\right)$$

$$V'(r) = \pi(20r - 10r^2)$$

$$0 = 10\pi r(2 - r)$$

$$r = 0 \qquad r = 2$$

The endpoints of the interval are $r = 0$ and $r = 3$. Since $V(0) = V(3) = 0$, the maximum volume occurs when $r = 2$. The corresponding value of $h = 10 - \dfrac{10}{3}r = 10 - \dfrac{20}{3} = \dfrac{10}{3}$.

The maximum volume is $V = \pi r^2 h = \pi \cdot 2^2 \cdot \dfrac{10}{3} = \dfrac{40\pi}{3}$ in^3.

11.

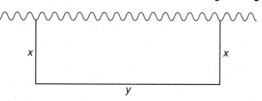

Since only three sides of the rectangle use fencing, $P = 2x + y$. Since the enclosed area is to be 1800 ft^2,

$$xy = 1800$$

$$y = \frac{1800}{x}$$

Substituting into the equation for P, we obtain P as a function of x.

$$P(x) = 2x + \frac{1800}{x} \qquad 0 < x < \infty$$

$P(x) = 2x + 1800x^{-1}$

$P'(x) = 2 - 1800x^{-2}$

$0 = 2 - \dfrac{1800}{x^2}$

> Clearly x cannot be negative, and x cannot equal 0, since this would yield a rectangle whose area is 0. Furthermore, x can be arbitrarily large, since it is always possible to find y sufficiently small to make $xy = 1800$.

$\dfrac{1800}{x^2} = 2$

$2x^2 = 1800$

$x^2 = 900$

$x = 30$

The corresponding value of $y = \dfrac{1800}{x} = \dfrac{1800}{30} = 60$ and the minimum amount of fencing needed is $2x + y = 120$ feet.

We may use the second derivative test to confirm that $x = 30$ corresponds to a relative minimum (optional).

$$P''(x) = 3600x^{-3} = \frac{3600}{x^3}$$

It is clear that $P''(30) > 0$, so we have a relative minimum at $x = 30$. Since it is the *only* relative extremum on the interval $(0, \infty)$, the function has its absolute minimum there.

12.

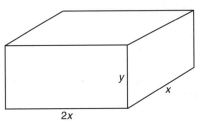

The amount of material needed to construct the box is the sum of the areas of its five sides (it's an *open* box). Since the base of the box is a rectangle x by $2x$, its area is $2x^2$. The front and back each have areas of $2xy$ and each side, left and right, has an area of xy. The total area is then

$$A = 2x^2 + 2xy + 2xy + xy + xy$$
$$= 2x^2 + 6xy$$

Since the volume ($l \times w \times h$) is 972 cm³,

$$(2x)(x)(y) = 972$$

$$2x^2y = 972$$

$$y = \frac{486}{x^2}$$

Substituting into the equation representing A,

$$A(x) = 2x^2 + 6x\left(\frac{486}{x^2}\right) \qquad 0 < x < \infty$$

$$= 2x^2 + \frac{2916}{x}$$

$$= 2x^2 + 2916x^{-1}$$

Next we differentiate and solve for the critical value:

$$A'(x) = 4x - 2916x^{-2}$$

$$0 = 4x - \frac{2916}{x^2}$$

$$\frac{2916}{x^2} = 4x$$

$$4x^3 = 2916$$

$$x^3 = 729$$

$$x = 9$$

The height of the box, determined from $y = \dfrac{486}{x^2}$, is $\dfrac{486}{81} = 6$. The dimensions for minimum surface area are 9 cm, 18 cm, and 6 cm. We confirm that this yields a minimum area (optional):

$$A''(x) = 4 + 5832x^{-3} = 4 + \frac{5832}{x^3}$$

Since $x = 9$ is a positive number, $A''(9) > 0$, and this value corresponds to a relative minimum. Since it is the only relative extremum on the interval $(0, \infty)$, it yields the absolute minimum.

13.

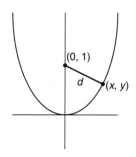

By symmetry, there appear to be *two* points closest to (0, 1). We shall find the point in the first quadrant.

Let (x, y) be an arbitrary point on the parabola. The distance between (x, y) and (0, 1) is

$$d = \sqrt{(x - 0)^2 + (y - 1)^2}$$

Since $y = x^2$ for all points on the parabola, the distance may be expressed as a function of x:

$$d(x) = \sqrt{x^2 + (x^2 - 1)^2}$$

$$= \sqrt{x^2 + x^4 - 2x^2 + 1}$$

$$= \sqrt{x^4 - x^2 + 1}$$

Rather than minimize $d(x)$, we consider $D = d^2$, observing that the minimum values of both d and D occur at the same value of x.

$$D(x) = x^4 - x^2 + 1$$

Since we are restricting our attention to the first quadrant, $0 \le x < \infty$.

$$D'(x) = 4x^3 - 2x$$

$$0 = 4x^3 - 2x$$

$$0 = 2x(2x^2 - 1)$$

Either $x = 0$ or $2x^2 - 1 = 0$, in which case $x = 1/\sqrt{2}$. ($x = -1/\sqrt{2}$ can be ignored.)

$$D''(x) = 12x^2 - 2$$

$$D''(0) = -2 < 0 \Rightarrow \text{ relative maximum at } 0$$

$$D''\left(\frac{1}{\sqrt{2}}\right) = 4 > 0 \Rightarrow \text{ relative minimum at } \frac{1}{\sqrt{2}}$$

Since $d(0) = 1$ and $d\left(\frac{1}{\sqrt{2}}\right) = \frac{3}{4}$, we conclude that the point closest to $(0, 1)$ in the first quadrant is $\left(\frac{1}{\sqrt{2}}, \frac{1}{2}\right)$. The corresponding point in the second quadrant is $\left(-\frac{1}{\sqrt{2}}, \frac{1}{2}\right)$.

14.

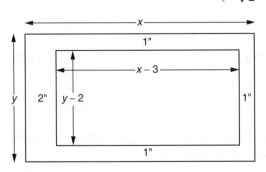

We represent the dimensions of the page by x and y as shown. The dimensions of the printed matter are then $x - 3$ and $y - 2$. (We could let x and y be the dimensions of the printed area, but this leads to a more difficult solution.)

The area to be maximized,

$$A = (x - 3)(y - 2)$$
$$= xy - 2x - 3y + 6$$

Since the area of the page is to be 96 in^2, $xy = 96$ and $y = \dfrac{96}{x}$. Substituting,

$$A(x) = 96 - 2x - 3\left(\frac{96}{x}\right) + 6$$

$$= 102 - 2x - 288x^{-1} \qquad 0 < x < \infty$$

Next we find the critical number.

$$A'(x) = -2 + 288x^{-2}$$

$$0 = -2 + \frac{288}{x^2}$$

$$2 = \frac{288}{x^2}$$

$$2x^2 = 288$$

$$x^2 = 144$$

$$x = 12$$

The corresponding value of y is $\dfrac{96}{x} = \dfrac{96}{12} = 8$. The dimensions of the page are 12 by 8 inches.

We can use the second derivative test to confirm a relative maximum (optional).

$$A'(x) = -2 + 288x^{-2}$$
$$A''(x) = -576x^{-3} = \frac{-576}{x^3}$$

It is clear that $A''(12) < 0$ so a relative maximum is confirmed. Since $x = 12$ is the only relative extremum on the interval $(0, \infty)$, it yields the absolute maximum.

15.

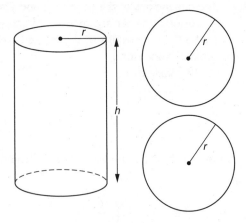

The surface area of the can consists of the lateral surface area and the area of the top and bottom circles.

$$S = \underbrace{2\pi r h}_{\substack{\text{lateral} \\ \text{surface} \\ \text{area}}} + \underbrace{2\pi r^2}_{\substack{\text{area of} \\ \text{top and} \\ \text{bottom}}}$$

Because the volume of the can must be 1000 in³,

$$\pi r^2 h = 1000$$

$$h = \frac{1000}{\pi r^2}$$

Substituting into the equation for S, we obtain a function of r.

$$S(r) = 2\pi r \left(\frac{1000}{\pi r^2} \right) + 2\pi r^2$$

$$= \frac{2000}{r} + 2\pi r^2$$

$$S(r) = 2000 r^{-1} + 2\pi r^2 \qquad 0 < r < \infty$$

We differentiate with respect to r and find the critical values by setting the derivative to 0.

$$S'(r) = -2000 r^{-2} + 4\pi r$$

$$0 = \frac{-2000}{r^2} + 4\pi r$$

$$\frac{2000}{r^2} = 4\pi r$$

$$4\pi r^3 = 2000$$

$$r^3 = \frac{500}{\pi}$$

$$r = \sqrt[3]{\frac{500}{\pi}} = 5\sqrt[3]{\frac{4}{\pi}}$$

The corresponding value of h is

$$h = \frac{1000}{\pi r^2} = \frac{1000}{\pi \left(5\sqrt[3]{\dfrac{4}{\pi}}\right)^2} = \frac{1000}{25\pi \dfrac{4^{2/3}}{\pi^{2/3}}}$$

$$= \frac{40}{\pi^{1/3} 4^{2/3}} = \frac{10 \cdot 4^{1/3}}{\pi^{1/3}} = 10\sqrt[3]{\frac{4}{\pi}}$$

We test the critical value using the second derivative test (optional).

$$S''(r) = 4000r^{-3} + 4\pi$$

$$= \frac{4000}{r^3} + 4\pi$$

Since the critical value is positive (its exact value is not needed), S'' is certainly positive at $5\sqrt[3]{\dfrac{4}{\pi}}$, so $S(r)$ has a relative minimum here. Since it is the only relative extremum on the interval $(0, \infty)$ it is the location of the absolute minimum.

16.

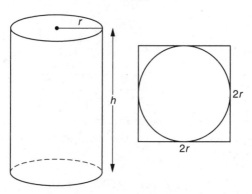

The material used in the construction of the can consists of three pieces. The area of the body of the can is $2\pi r h$ and the material used in the construction of the top or bottom is $(2r)^2$. (We must consider the wasted material as well as the material used for the circular end.)

Hence

$$A = 2\pi rh + (2r)^2 + (2r)^2$$

$$= 2\pi rh + 8r^2$$

Since the volume of the can is to be 1000 in³, $\pi r^2 h = 1000$ and $h = \dfrac{1000}{\pi r^2}$. It follows that

$$A(r) = 2\pi r \left(\frac{1000}{\pi r^2} \right) + 8r^2$$

$$= \frac{2000}{r} + 8r^2$$

$$= 2000r^{-1} + 8r^2 \qquad 0 < r < \infty$$

Differentiating and finding the critical number,

$$A'(r) = -2000r^{-2} + 16r$$

$$0 = \frac{-2000}{r^2} + 16r$$

$$\frac{2000}{r^2} = 16r$$

$$16r^3 = 2000$$

$$r^3 = 125$$

$$r = 5$$

$$h = \frac{1000}{\pi r^2} = \frac{1000}{25\pi} = \frac{40}{\pi} \text{ in}$$

We use the second derivative test to confirm our suspicions that this is the radius that requires the minimum amount of material (optional).

$$A''(r) = 4000r^{-3} + 16$$

$$= \frac{4000}{r^3} + 16$$

Since $A''(5) > 0$ (exact calculation is unnecessary), $r = 5$ yields a relative minimum. Since it is the only relative extremum on $(0, \infty)$, it gives the absolute minimum as well.

17.

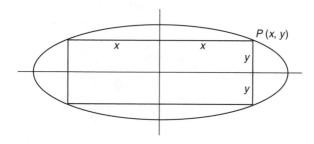

Let (x, y) represent the point P in the first quadrant where the rectangle meets the ellipse. Then the dimensions of the rectangle are $2x$ by $2y$ so its area $A = 4xy$. Since P lies on the ellipse, its coordinates must satisfy the equation of the ellipse, $\dfrac{x^2}{200} + \dfrac{y^2}{50} = 1$. We solve for y:

$$\frac{y^2}{50} = 1 - \frac{x^2}{200}$$

$$y^2 = 50 - \frac{x^2}{4}$$

$$= \frac{200 - x^2}{4}$$

$$y = \frac{\sqrt{200 - x^2}}{2}$$

The area may be expressed as a function of x by substitution into $A = 4xy$:

$$A(x) = 4x \frac{\sqrt{200 - x^2}}{2}$$

$$= 2x\sqrt{200 - x^2} \qquad 0 \leq x \leq \sqrt{200}$$

Rather than deal with this function directly, it is more convenient to consider its square. We can call it $F(x)$. The value of x that maximizes $F(x)$ will maximize $A(x)$.

$$F(x) = [A(x)]^2$$
$$= 4x^2(200 - x^2)$$
$$= 800x^2 - 4x^4$$
$$F'(x) = 1600x - 16x^3$$
$$0 = 1600x - 16x^3$$
$$0 = 16x(100 - x^2)$$
$$x = 0 \qquad x = 10$$

Since $F(0) = F(\sqrt{200}) = 0$, it follows that the maximum area occurs when $x = 10$ and $y = \dfrac{\sqrt{200 - x^2}}{2} = 5$. $A_{max} = 4xy = 200$.

Chapter 5

Trigonometric Functions

In Chapters 3 and 4 we discussed techniques for solving related rates and maximum-minimum problems. These extend directly to problems involving trigonometric functions. The use of trigonometry can often simplify the solution of word problems significantly.

The derivatives of the trigonometric functions play an important role in the solution of these problems.

$$\frac{d}{dx}\sin x = \cos x \qquad \frac{d}{dx}\cos x = -\sin x$$
$$\frac{d}{dx}\tan x = \sec^2 x \qquad \frac{d}{dx}\cot x = -\csc^2 x$$
$$\frac{d}{dx}\sec x = \sec x \tan x \qquad \frac{d}{dx}\csc x = -\csc x \cot x$$

It is important to remember that these derivative formulas are correct only if x is expressed in radian measure. Therefore, any angles or rates expressed in degrees should be converted to radians. This can be easily accomplished by remembering that π radians is equivalent to $180°$.

The Pythagorean identities are useful in simplifying trigonometric expressions:

$$\sin^2 x + \cos^2 x = 1 \qquad \tan^2 x + 1 = \sec^2 x \qquad \cot^2 x + 1 = \csc^2 x$$

129

The law of cosines is often needed when dealing with problems involving triangles other than right triangles.

$$c^2 = a^2 + b^2 - 2ab\cos\theta$$

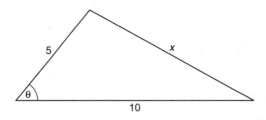

Observe that if $\theta = \pi/2$, the law of cosines reduces to the theorem of Pythagoras: $c^2 = a^2 + b^2$. Other trigonometric identities will be discussed as needed in the examples that follow.

Related Rates

EXAMPLE I

Two sides of a triangle are 5 and 10 inches, respectively. The angle between them is increasing at the rate of 5° per minute. How fast is the third side of the triangle growing when the angle is 60° ?

Solution

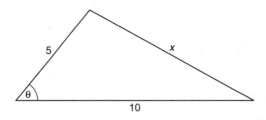

Let θ represent the angle between the sides of length 5 and 10 and let x represent the length of the third side of the triangle. In any calculus problem involving derivatives, all angles and rates must be expressed in radian measure.

Given: $\dfrac{d\theta}{dt} = \dfrac{\pi}{36}$ radians per minute   Find: $\dfrac{dx}{dt}$ when $\theta = \dfrac{\pi}{3}$

$\left(5° = \dfrac{180°}{36} = \dfrac{\pi}{36}\text{ radians}\right)$ $\left(60° = \dfrac{\pi}{3}\text{ radians}\right)$

By the law of cosines,

$$x^2 = 5^2 + 10^2 - 2 \cdot 5 \cdot 10 \cdot \cos\theta$$

$$x^2 = 125 - 100\cos\theta$$

Differentiating with respect to t,

$$2x\frac{dx}{dt} = 0 - 100(-\sin\theta)\frac{d\theta}{dt}$$

$$x\frac{dx}{dt} = 50\sin\theta\frac{d\theta}{dt}$$

We need the value of x when $\theta = \dfrac{\pi}{3}$. Since $x^2 = 125 - 100\cos\theta$, when $\theta = \dfrac{\pi}{3}$,

$$x^2 = 125 - 50 = 75$$

$$x = \sqrt{75} = 5\sqrt{3}$$

$$\sin\frac{\pi}{3} = \frac{\sqrt{3}}{2}$$
$$\cos\frac{\pi}{3} = \frac{1}{2}$$

Substituting,

$$5\sqrt{3}\frac{dx}{dt} = 50 \cdot \frac{\sqrt{3}}{2} \cdot \frac{\pi}{36}$$

$$5\sqrt{3}\frac{dx}{dt} = \frac{25\pi\sqrt{3}}{36}$$

$$\frac{dx}{dt} = \frac{5\pi}{36} \text{ in/min}$$

EXAMPLE 2

A kite is flying 100 ft above the ground, moving in a strictly horizontal direction at a rate of 10 ft/sec. How fast is the angle between the string and the horizontal changing when there is 300 ft of string out?

Solution

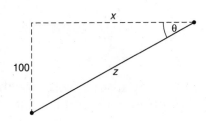

Given: $\dfrac{dx}{dt} = 10$ Find: $\dfrac{d\theta}{dt}$ when $z = 300$

We could use the relationship $\tan \theta = \dfrac{100}{x}$, but it will be easier to deal with x if it appears in the numerator of the fraction. We prefer the *cotangent* function.

$$\cot \theta = \frac{x}{100}$$

$$x = 100 \cot \theta$$

It follows that

$$\frac{dx}{dt} = 100(-\csc^2 \theta)\frac{d\theta}{dt}$$

$$\frac{dx}{dt} = \frac{-100}{\sin^2 \theta} \cdot \frac{d\theta}{dt}$$

Solving for $\dfrac{d\theta}{dt}$,

$$\frac{d\theta}{dt} = \frac{-\sin^2 \theta}{100} \cdot \frac{dx}{dt}$$

From the diagram we can see that $\sin \theta = \dfrac{1}{3}$ when $z = 300$.

$$\frac{d\theta}{dt} = -\frac{1/9}{100} \cdot 10$$

$$= -\frac{1}{90}$$

θ is decreasing at the rate of $\dfrac{1}{90}$ rad/sec.

EXAMPLE 3

A police car is 20 ft away from a long straight wall. Its beacon, rotating 1 revolution per second, shines a beam of light on the wall. How fast is the beam moving when it is closest to the police car?

Solution

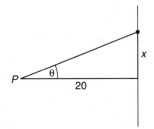

Given: $\dfrac{d\theta}{dt} = 2\pi$ (Since 1 revolution is 2π radians, the value of

$$\frac{d\theta}{dt} = 2\pi \text{ rad/sec.})$$

Find: $\dfrac{dx}{dt}$ when $\theta = 0$ (The beam is closest to the police car when $\theta = 0$.)

$$\tan\theta = \frac{x}{20}$$

$$x = 20\tan\theta$$

$$\frac{dx}{dt} = 20\sec^2\theta \cdot \frac{d\theta}{dt}$$

Substituting $\theta = 0$ and $\dfrac{d\theta}{dt} = 2\pi$ we compute $\dfrac{dx}{dt}$:

$$\frac{dx}{dt} = 20 \cdot 1^2 \cdot 2\pi = 40\pi \text{ ft/sec.}$$

EXAMPLE 4

A runner and his trainer are standing together on a circular track of radius 100 meters. When the trainer gives a signal, the runner starts to run around the track at a speed of 10 m/s. How fast is the distance between the runner and the trainer increasing when the runner has run $\dfrac{1}{4}$ of the way around the track?

SOLUTION

Let x represent the (straight-line) distance between the runner and the trainer and let s represent the distance run around the track.

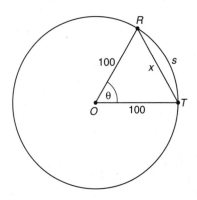

The angle formed by the two radii as shown in the diagram is labeled θ.

Given: $\dfrac{ds}{dt} = 10$ Find: $\dfrac{dx}{dt}$ when $\theta = \dfrac{\pi}{2}$

By the law of cosines,

$$x^2 = 100^2 + 100^2 - 2(100)(100) \cos \theta$$
$$x^2 = 20{,}000 - 20{,}000 \cos \theta$$

Differentiating,

$$2x\frac{dx}{dt} = 20{,}000 \sin \theta \frac{d\theta}{dt}$$

$$x\frac{dx}{dt} = 10{,}000 \sin \theta \frac{d\theta}{dt}$$

To compute $\dfrac{dx}{dt}$ when $\theta = \dfrac{\pi}{2}$, we need the values of x and $\dfrac{d\theta}{dt}$.

When the runner has run $\frac{1}{4}$ of the way around the track, $\theta = \pi/2$. Triangle ORT then becomes a right triangle.

$$x^2 = 100^2 + 100^2 \qquad\qquad s = r\,\theta$$

$$= 20{,}000 \qquad\qquad s = 100\,\theta$$

$$x = 100\sqrt{2} \qquad\qquad \frac{ds}{dt} = 100\frac{d\theta}{dt}$$

$$10 = 100\frac{d\theta}{dt}$$

$$\frac{d\theta}{dt} = \frac{1}{10}$$

We can now compute $\dfrac{dx}{dt}$:

$$x\frac{dx}{dt} = 10{,}000 \sin\theta\, \frac{d\theta}{dt}$$

$$100\sqrt{2}\frac{dx}{dt} = 10{,}000 \cdot \overbrace{\sin\left(\frac{\pi}{2}\right)}^{1} \cdot \left(\frac{1}{10}\right)$$

$$100\sqrt{2}\frac{dx}{dt} = 1000$$

$$\frac{dx}{dt} = \frac{1000}{100\sqrt{2}} = \frac{10}{\sqrt{2}} = 5\sqrt{2}\ \text{m/sec}$$

Maximum-Minimum Problems

Many maximum-minimum problems are conveniently solved by introducing trigonometric functions.

EXAMPLE 5

What is the largest possible area of a triangle, two of whose sides are a and b?

Solution

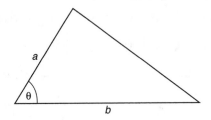

Let θ represent the angle between the two sides. The area of the triangle is

$$A(\theta) = \frac{1}{2}ab \, \sin\theta \qquad 0 \le \theta \le \pi$$

Since a and b are constants, $A'(\theta) = \frac{1}{2}ab\cos\theta$. Setting the derivative equal to 0 and solving, we obtain

$$0 = \frac{1}{2}ab\cos\theta$$

$$0 = \cos\theta$$

$$\theta = \frac{\pi}{2}$$

Since $A(\theta)$ is a continuous function and $A(0) = A(\pi) = 0$, the absolute maximum area occurs when $\theta = \frac{\pi}{2}$ (a right angle). Since $\sin\frac{\pi}{2} = 1$, $A_{max} = A\left(\frac{\pi}{2}\right) = \frac{1}{2}ab$.

EXAMPLE 6

A man at point A on the shore of a circular lake of radius 1 mile wants to reach point B on the shore diametrically opposite A. If he can row a boat 3 mi/h and jog 6 mi/h, at what angle θ with the diameter should he row in order to reach B in the shortest possible time?

Solution

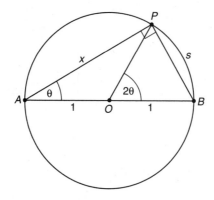

Let P be the point where the boat reaches the shore. Since triangle APB is inscribed in a semicircle, it is a right triangle with hypotenuse 2.

$$\frac{x}{2} = \cos\theta$$

$$x = 2\cos\theta$$

A geometry theorem says that a central angle is measured by its intercepted arc, while an inscribed angle is measured by half its intercepted arc. Since $\overset{\frown}{PB}$ is the intercepted arc for both $\angle POB$ and $\angle PAB$, it follows that $\angle POB$ is twice $\angle PAB$ or 2θ. The arc length $s = r(2\theta) = 2\theta$.

If r is the constant rate of a moving object and d is the distance traveled, the time of travel $t = \dfrac{d}{r}$. It follows that the time to make the journey from A to B as a function of θ is

$$t = t_{\text{row}} + t_{\text{jog}}$$

$$t = \frac{x}{3} + \frac{s}{6}$$

$$t(\theta) = \frac{2\cos\theta}{3} + \frac{2\theta}{6}$$

$$= \frac{2}{3}\cos\theta + \frac{\theta}{3} \qquad 0 \le \theta \le \frac{\pi}{2}$$

137

We differentiate to find the critical numbers.

$$t'(\theta) = -\frac{2}{3}\sin\theta + \frac{1}{3}$$

$$0 = -\frac{2}{3}\sin\theta + \frac{1}{3}$$

$$\frac{2}{3}\sin\theta = \frac{1}{3}$$

$$\sin\theta = \frac{1}{2}$$

$$\theta = \frac{\pi}{6}$$

Since $t(\theta) = \frac{2}{3}\cos\theta + \frac{\theta}{3}$ is a continuous function of θ, the absolute minimum may occur at the critical number or at an endpoint of the interval $[0, \pi/2]$.

$$t(0) = \frac{2}{3} \approx 0.667$$

$$t\left(\frac{\pi}{6}\right) = \frac{2}{3}\cdot\frac{\sqrt{3}}{2} + \frac{\pi}{18} = \frac{6\sqrt{3}+\pi}{18} \approx 0.752$$

$$t\left(\frac{\pi}{2}\right) = \frac{\pi}{6} \approx 0.524 \qquad \leftarrow\text{absolute minimum}$$

To minimize the time to get from A to B, the man should jog completely around the lake.

EXAMPLE 7

Two vehicles, A and B, start at point P and travel east at rates of 10 km/h and 30 km/h, respectively. An observer at Q, 1 km north of P, is able to observe both vehicles. What is the maximum angle of sight between the observer's view of A and B?

Solution

Let θ represent the angle of sight. It will be convenient to introduce angles α and β as shown in the figure below.

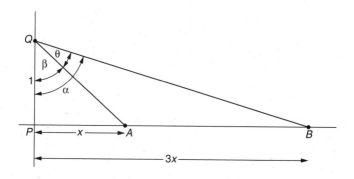

Since B travels three times as fast as A, PB will be $3x$ when $PA = x$. Since $|PQ| = 1$, $\tan \alpha = 3x$ and $\tan \beta = x$. Since $\theta = \alpha - \beta$, it follows that

$$\tan \theta = \tan(\alpha - \beta)$$

$$= \frac{\tan \alpha - \tan \beta}{1 + \tan \alpha \tan \beta}$$

$$= \frac{3x - x}{1 + (3x)x}$$

$$\tan \theta = \frac{2x}{1 + 3x^2} \qquad 0 \le x < \infty$$

$$\tan(\alpha + \beta) = \frac{\tan \alpha + \tan \beta}{1 - \tan \alpha \tan \beta}$$

$$\tan(\alpha - \beta) = \frac{\tan \alpha - \tan \beta}{1 + \tan \alpha \tan \beta}$$

Since we want to maximize θ, we need $\dfrac{d\theta}{dx}$.

$$\sec^2 \theta \cdot \frac{d\theta}{dx} = \frac{(1 + 3x^2)(2) - (2x)(6x)}{(1 + 3x^2)^2}$$

$$= \frac{2 - 6x^2}{(1 + 3x^2)^2}$$

139

Setting $\dfrac{d\theta}{dx} = 0$,

$$0 = \frac{2 - 6x^2}{(1 + 3x^2)^2}$$

$$0 = 2 - 6x^2$$

$$6x^2 = 2$$

$$x = \frac{1}{\sqrt{3}} = \frac{\sqrt{3}}{3}$$

Since $\sec^2 \theta > 0$, $\dfrac{d\theta}{dx}$ is positive if $x < \dfrac{\sqrt{3}}{3}$ and negative if $x > \dfrac{\sqrt{3}}{3}$. By the first derivative test, θ has a relative maximum at $\sqrt{3}/3$. Since it is the only relative extremum on the interval $[0, \infty)$, it must give the absolute maximum.

Since $\tan \theta = \dfrac{2x}{1 + 3x^2}$, the value $x = \dfrac{\sqrt{3}}{3}$ gives

$$\tan \theta = \frac{\dfrac{2\sqrt{3}}{3}}{1 + 3 \cdot \dfrac{1}{3}} = \frac{\sqrt{3}}{3}$$

The corresponding value of θ is $\pi/6$. The maximum angle of sight is $30°$.

EXAMPLE 8

Find the maximum area of a rectangle circumscribed about a fixed rectangle of length 8 and width 4.

Solution

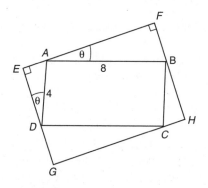

Let $\theta = \angle FAB$ as shown in the figure. By geometry, $\angle EDA = \theta$ as well. The distances $|EA| = 4\sin\theta$, $|AF| = 8\cos\theta$, $|ED| = 4\cos\theta$, and $|DG| = |FB| = 8\sin\theta$. The area of the circumscribed rectangle is the product $(|ED| + |DG|)(|EA| + |AF|)$. Hence

$$A(\theta) = (4\cos\theta + 8\sin\theta)(4\sin\theta + 8\cos\theta)$$

$$= 32\cos^2\theta + 32\sin^2\theta + 80\sin\theta\cos\theta$$

$$= 32 + 40\sin 2\theta \qquad 0 \le \theta \le \frac{\pi}{2}$$

$$A'(\theta) = 80\cos 2\theta$$

$$0 = 80\cos 2\theta$$

$$0 = \cos 2\theta$$

$$2\theta = \frac{\pi}{2}$$

$$\theta = \frac{\pi}{4}$$

$$\boxed{\sin^2\theta + \cos^2\theta = 1}$$
$$\sin 2\theta = 2\sin\theta\cos\theta$$

Observe that $A(\theta)$ is a continuous function. Since $A(0) = A(\pi/2) = 32$ and $A(\pi/4) = 72$, the maximum area of 72 in^2 occurs when $\theta = \pi/4$.

Supplementary Problems

1. A ladder 10 ft long is resting against the side of a building. If the foot of the ladder slips away from the wall at the rate of 2 ft/min, how fast is the angle between the ladder and the building changing when the foot of the ladder is 6 ft away from the building?

2. Two sides of a triangle are 3 in and 4 in long. If the angle between them is increasing at the rate of 2° per second, how fast is the area of the triangle increasing when the angle is 45°?

3. A television camera is located 5000 ft from the base of a rocket launching pad. The camera is designed to follow the vertical path of the rocket. If the rocket's speed is 500 ft/sec when it has risen 2000 ft, how fast is the camera's angle of elevation changing at this instant?

4. A lighthouse is situated 2 km away from a beach and its beacon revolves at the rate of 3 revolutions per minute. If P is the point on the beach nearest the lighthouse, how fast is the beam of light moving along the beach when it is 1 km from P?

5. Two corridors of widths a and b intersect at right angles. What is the length of the longest pipe that can be carried horizontally around the corner?

6. A painting of height 3 ft hangs on a wall with the bottom of the painting 6 ft above the floor. How far from the wall should Lindsay, whose eyes are 5 ft from the floor, stand in order to get the best view of the painting? (The best view occurs when the angle of vision from the bottom to the top of the painting is maximized.)

Solutions to Supplementary Problems

1.

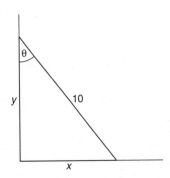

142

Given: $\dfrac{dx}{dt} = 2$ Find: $\dfrac{d\theta}{dt}$ when $x = 6$

$$\frac{x}{10} = \sin\theta$$

$$x = 10\sin\theta$$

$$\frac{dx}{dt} = 10\cos\theta\frac{d\theta}{dt}$$

At the instant in question, $x = 6$. By the theorem of Pythagoras, $y = 8$. It follows that $\cos\theta = \dfrac{8}{10}$.

$$2 = 10\cdot\frac{8}{10}\cdot\frac{d\theta}{dt}$$

$$2 = 8\frac{d\theta}{dt}$$

$$\frac{d\theta}{dt} = \frac{1}{4}$$

The angle is increasing at the rate of $\dfrac{1}{4}$ radian per minute.

2.

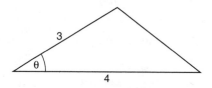

$2°$ per second is equivalent to $\pi/90$ radians per second.
$45° = \pi/4$ radians.

Given: $\dfrac{d\theta}{dt} = \dfrac{\pi}{90}$ Find: $\dfrac{dA}{dt}$ when $\theta = \pi/4$

The area of a triangle with sides a and b and included angle θ is $\dfrac{1}{2}ab\sin\theta$. Since $a = 3$ and $b = 4$, this reduces to $A = 6\sin\theta$.

$$A = 6 \sin \theta$$

$$\frac{dA}{dt} = 6 \cos \theta \frac{d\theta}{dt}$$

When $\theta = \pi/4$

$$\frac{dA}{dt} = 6 \cos \frac{\pi}{4} \cdot \left(\frac{\pi}{90} \right)$$

$$= 6 \cdot \frac{\sqrt{2}}{2} \cdot \frac{\pi}{90}$$

$$= \frac{\pi \sqrt{2}}{30}$$

The area of the triangle is increasing at the rate of $\dfrac{\pi \sqrt{2}}{30}$ in²/sec.

3.

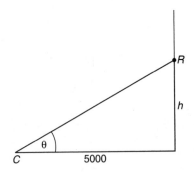

Given: $\dfrac{dh}{dt} = 500$ when $h = 2000$ Find: $\dfrac{d\theta}{dt}$ when $h = 2000$

$$\frac{h}{5000} = \tan \theta$$

$$h = 5000 \tan \theta$$

$$\frac{dh}{dt} = 5000 \sec^2 \theta \frac{d\theta}{dt}$$

$\tan \theta = \dfrac{h}{5000}$. When $h = 2000$, $\tan \theta = \dfrac{2}{5}$. Since

$\sec^2 \theta = \tan^2 \theta + 1$, $\sec^2 \theta = \dfrac{4}{25} + 1 = \dfrac{29}{25}$.

144

It follows that

$$500 = 5000 \cdot \frac{29}{25} \cdot \frac{d\theta}{dt}$$

$$500 = 5800 \frac{d\theta}{dt}$$

$$\frac{d\theta}{dt} = \frac{500}{5800} = \frac{5}{58} \text{ rad/sec}$$

In terms of degrees $\dfrac{d\theta}{dt} = \dfrac{5}{58} \cdot \dfrac{180}{\pi} \approx 4.94$ degrees/sec

4.

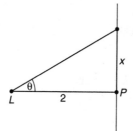

Given: $\dfrac{d\theta}{dt} = 6\pi$ rad/min $\qquad$ Find: $\dfrac{dx}{dt}$ when $x = 1$
(3 revolutions $= 6\pi$ radians)

$$\frac{x}{2} = \tan\theta$$

$$x = 2\tan\theta$$

$$\frac{dx}{dt} = 2\sec^2\theta \frac{d\theta}{dt}$$

When $x = 1$, $\tan\theta = \dfrac{1}{2}$. Since $\sec^2\theta = \tan^2\theta + 1$, it follows that $\sec^2\theta = \dfrac{5}{4}$.

$$\frac{dx}{dt} = 2 \cdot \frac{5}{4} \cdot 6\pi$$

$$= 15\pi \text{ km/min}$$

5.

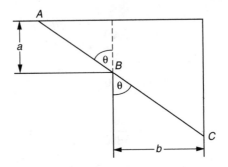

Let θ be the angle between the pipe and the vertical as shown in the diagram.

$$\frac{|AB|}{a} = \sec\theta \qquad \frac{|BC|}{b} = \csc\theta$$

$$|AB| = a\sec\theta \qquad |BC| = b\csc\theta$$

If L represents the length of the pipe,

$$L = |AB| + |BC|$$

$$L(\theta) = a\sec\theta + b\csc\theta$$

We differentiate with respect to θ and find the critical value of this function.

$$L'(\theta) = a\sec\theta\tan\theta - b\csc\theta\cot\theta$$

$$0 = a\sec\theta\tan\theta - b\csc\theta\cot\theta$$

$$a\sec\theta\tan\theta = b\csc\theta\cot\theta$$

$$a\frac{\sin\theta}{\cos^2\theta} = b\frac{\cos\theta}{\sin^2\theta}$$

$$a\sin^3\theta = b\cos^3\theta$$

$$\tan\theta = \frac{\sin\theta}{\cos\theta}$$

$$\cot\theta = \frac{\cos\theta}{\sin\theta}$$

$$\sec\theta = \frac{1}{\cos\theta}$$

$$\csc\theta = \frac{1}{\sin\theta}$$

$$\frac{\sin^3 \theta}{\cos^3 \theta} = \frac{b}{a}$$

$$\tan^3 \theta = \frac{b}{a}$$

$$\tan \theta = \sqrt[3]{\frac{b}{a}} = \frac{b^{1/3}}{a^{1/3}}$$

Note: The angle θ such that $\tan \theta = b^{1/3}/a^{1/3}$ is actually the angle corresponding to the pipe of *minimum* length that will *not* fit around the corner. As $\theta \to 0$ or $\theta \to \pi/2$, $L \to \infty$.

$$\sec^2 \theta = \tan^2 \theta + 1 \qquad \csc^2 \theta = \cot^2 \theta + 1$$

$$= \frac{b^{2/3}}{a^{2/3}} + 1 \qquad\qquad = \frac{a^{2/3}}{b^{2/3}} + 1$$

$$= \frac{a^{2/3} + b^{2/3}}{a^{2/3}} \qquad\qquad = \frac{a^{2/3} + b^{2/3}}{b^{2/3}}$$

$$\sec \theta = \frac{\sqrt{a^{2/3} + b^{2/3}}}{a^{1/3}} \qquad \csc \theta = \frac{\sqrt{a^{2/3} + b^{2/3}}}{b^{1/3}}$$

$$L = a \sec \theta + b \csc \theta$$

$$= a \frac{\sqrt{a^{2/3} + b^{2/3}}}{a^{1/3}} + b \frac{\sqrt{a^{2/3} + b^{2/3}}}{b^{1/3}}$$

$$= a^{2/3} \sqrt{a^{2/3} + b^{2/3}} + b^{2/3} \sqrt{a^{2/3} + b^{2/3}}$$

$$= (a^{2/3} + b^{2/3}) \sqrt{a^{2/3} + b^{2/3}}$$

$$= (a^{2/3} + b^{2/3})^{3/2}$$

6. Let x be the distance Lindsay stands from the wall.

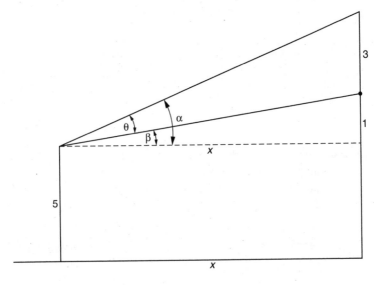

Let α and β be as shown. $\tan \alpha = \dfrac{4}{x}$ and $\beta = \dfrac{1}{x}$. Since $\theta = \alpha - \beta$,

$$\tan \theta = \tan(\alpha - \beta)$$

$$= \frac{\tan \alpha - \tan \beta}{1 + \tan \alpha \tan \beta}$$

$$= \frac{\dfrac{4}{x} - \dfrac{1}{x}}{1 + \dfrac{4}{x^2}}$$

$$= \frac{\dfrac{3}{x}}{1 + \dfrac{4}{x^2}}$$

$$\tan \theta = \frac{3x}{x^2 + 4}$$

Since we want to minimize θ, we need $\dfrac{d\theta}{dx}$. Differentiating with respect to x,

$$\sec^2\theta \frac{d\theta}{dx} = \frac{(x^2+4)3 - 3x(2x)}{(x^2+4)^2}$$

$$= \frac{12 - 3x^2}{(x^2+4)^2}$$

To find the critical value, we set $\dfrac{d\theta}{dx} = 0$

$$0 = \frac{12 - 3x^2}{(x^2+4)^2}$$

$$0 = 12 - 3x^2$$

$$3x^2 = 12$$

$$x^2 = 4$$

$$x = 2$$

Since $\sec^2 x > 0$, $\dfrac{d\theta}{dx} > 0$ if $0 < x < 2$ and $\dfrac{d\theta}{dx} < 0$ if $x > 2$. By the first derivative test, $x = 2$ is the location of a relative maximum. Since it is the only relative extremum on the interval $(0, \infty)$, $x = 2$ is the location of the absolute maximum. Lindsay should stand 2 ft from the wall.

Chapter 6

Exponential Functions

If b is positive and x is real, the function $f(x) = b^x$ is called an exponential function. If the base of the exponential is $e \approx 2.71828$, the function is known as the *natural* exponential function. Its inverse is the natural logarithm function, usually represented as $\ln x$.

Listed below are some of the basic properties of the natural exponential and logarithm functions.

$$y = e^x \text{ if and only if } x = \ln y$$

$e^0 = 1$	$\ln 1 = 0$
$e^1 = e$	$\ln e = 1$
$e^{x+y} = e^x e^y$	$\ln xy = \ln x + \ln y$
$e^{x-y} = \dfrac{e^x}{e^y}$	$\ln \dfrac{x}{y} = \ln x - \ln y$
$(e^x)^y = e^{xy}$	$\ln x^y = y \ln x$

It is also useful to remember that as direct consequences of the above properties, $\ln \dfrac{1}{x} = -\ln x$ and $-\ln \dfrac{x}{y} = \ln \dfrac{y}{x}$. Because e^x and $\ln x$ are inverse functions $e^{\ln x} = x$ and $\ln(e^x) = x$.

The graphs of the exponential functions e^x and e^{-x} are shown below for reference. These functions play a fundamental role in problems involving exponential growth and decay. Observe that $\lim\limits_{x \to -\infty} e^x = 0$ and $\lim\limits_{x \to \infty} e^{-x} = 0$.

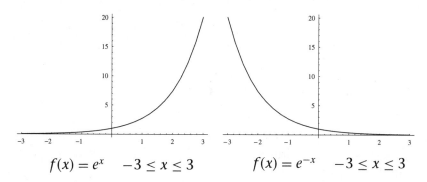

$$f(x) = e^x \quad -3 \le x \le 3 \qquad f(x) = e^{-x} \quad -3 \le x \le 3$$

Exponential-Growth and Decay

If a substance grows or decays at a rate proportional to its size, its growth may be described by the equation

$$\frac{dy}{dt} = ky$$

where y is the amount of the substance and k is the constant of proportionality. Positive values of k correspond to growth and negative values correspond to decay.

To solve for y, we rewrite the equation in the form

$$\frac{1}{y}\frac{dy}{dt} = k$$

from which it follows by the chain rule that

$$\frac{d}{dt}\ln y = k$$

Antidifferentiating, we get

$$\ln y = kt + C$$

If $y = y_0$ when $t = 0$, it follows that $\ln y_0 = C$ and we may write

$$\ln y = kt + \ln y_0$$
$$\ln y - \ln y_0 = kt$$
$$\ln \frac{y}{y_0} = kt$$
$$\frac{y}{y_0} = e^{kt}$$

$$\boxed{y = y_0 e^{kt}}$$

If the value of y_0 is known and the value of k can be determined, we can represent the amount of the substance as a function of time.

EXAMPLE I

A bacteria culture has an initial population of 500. After 4 hours the population has grown to 1000. Assuming the culture grows at a rate proportional to the size of the population, find a function representing the population size after t hours and determine the size of the population after 6 hours.

Solution

Let $y(t)$ represent the size of the bacteria population after t hours. Since the rate of growth of the population is proportional to the population size, it follows from the above discussion that

$$y(t) = y_0 e^{kt}$$
$$y(t) = 500 e^{kt}$$

Since $y(4) = 1000$, it follows that

$$1000 = 500 e^{4k}$$
$$2 = e^{4k}$$
$$4k = \ln 2$$

Recall that $y = \ln x \Leftrightarrow x = e^y$

$$k = \frac{1}{4} \ln 2$$

Thus

$$y(t) = 500e^{\left(\frac{1}{4}\ln 2\right)t}$$
$$= 500e^{\frac{t}{4}\ln 2}$$
$$= 500(e^{\ln 2})^{\frac{t}{4}}$$
$$= 500(2)^{\frac{t}{4}}$$

To determine the population size after 6 hours ($t = 6$), we compute $y(6) = 500(2)^{1.5} \approx 1414$.

Exponential decay occurs when a substance deteriorates with time. If the rate of decay is proportional to the amount of substance present, its mass satisfies the equation

$$\frac{dy}{dt} = -ky$$

In this equation, k is a positive constant. The minus sign preceding it indicates that the rate of change is negative, i.e., the mass is decreasing. Solving this equation in the manner described above, we are led to the solution $\boxed{y = y_0e^{-kt}}$.

EXAMPLE 2

A radioactive substance has a mass of 100 mg. After 10 years it has decayed to a mass of 75 mg. What will the mass of the substance be after another 10 years?

Solution

Let $y(t)$ represent the mass of the substance after t years. We know $y(0) = 100$ and $y(10) = 75$. We wish to determine the value of $y(20)$.

$$y(t) = y_0e^{-kt}$$
$$y(t) = 100e^{-kt}$$

First we need to determine k. This can be done by substituting $t = 10$.

$$y(10) = 100e^{-10k}$$

$$75 = 100e^{-10k}$$

$$\frac{3}{4} = e^{-10k}$$

$$-10k = \ln\frac{3}{4}$$

$$10k = \ln\frac{4}{3}$$

$$k = \frac{1}{10}\ln\frac{4}{3} \qquad \leftarrow k \text{ is a } \textit{positive} \text{ number}$$

The function $y(t)$ can now be determined.

$$y(t) = 100e^{-\left(\frac{1}{10}\ln\frac{4}{3}\right)t}$$
$$= 100e^{-\frac{t}{10}\ln\frac{4}{3}}$$
$$= 100(e^{\ln\frac{4}{3}})^{-\frac{t}{10}}$$
$$= 100\left(\frac{4}{3}\right)^{-\frac{t}{10}}$$

To solve the problem, let $t = 20$.

$$y(20) = 100\left(\frac{4}{3}\right)^{-2}$$

$$= 100\left(\frac{3}{4}\right)^{2}$$

$$= 100 \cdot \frac{9}{16}$$

$$= 56.25 \text{ mg}$$

The *half-life* of a radioactive substance is the time it takes for the substance to decay to *half* its original mass. If $y(t) = y_0 e^{-kt}$, the half-life is the value of t for which $y(t) = \frac{1}{2}y_0$.

$$\frac{1}{2}y_0 = y_0 e^{-kt}$$

$$\frac{1}{2} = e^{-kt}$$

The value of y_0 is irrelevant for this calculation.

$$-kt = \ln\frac{1}{2}$$

$$kt = \ln 2$$

$$t = \frac{\ln 2}{k}$$

We shall represent the half-life of a substance by the letter T: $T = \frac{\ln 2}{k}$. If the half-life is known, the value of $k = \frac{\ln 2}{T}$. The next example illustrates how knowledge of the half-life of a substance can help us solve exponential decay problems.

EXAMPLE 3

The half-life of ^{14}C (carbon-14) is 5730 years. How long will it take a 100-mg sample of ^{14}C to decay to 90 mg?

Solution

$$y(t) = y_0 e^{-kt}$$

$$k = \frac{\ln 2}{T} = \frac{\ln 2}{5730}$$

Although k may be approximated by 0.000121, such approximations often lead to error. We prefer the exact value. Using this value of k, we proceed to solve the problem.

$$y(t) = y_0 e^{-kt}$$

$$y(t) = 100 e^{-\left(\frac{\ln 2}{5730}\right)t}$$

To determine the time to reduce to 90 grams, we let $y(t) = 90$.

$$90 = 100e^{-\left(\frac{\ln 2}{5730}\right)t}$$

$$0.9 = e^{-\left(\frac{\ln 2}{5730}\right)t}$$

$$-\left(\frac{\ln 2}{5730}\right)t = \ln 0.9$$

$$t = -\frac{5730(\ln 0.9)}{\ln 2}$$

$$t \approx 870.98$$

It will take approximately 871 years to decay to 90 mg.

^{14}C, a radioactive isotope of carbon, as well as ^{12}C, a stable isotope, are both found in the atmosphere. Plants, which absorb carbon dioxide from the air, have the same ratio of ^{14}C to ^{12}C as the atmosphere. The same is true for animals that eat plants.

When a plant or an animal dies, it no longer absorbs carbon dioxide. Its ^{14}C decays but its ^{12}C does not. By measuring the ratio of ^{14}C to ^{12}C, scientists can approximate the age of a fossil by comparing this number to the known ratio of ^{14}C to ^{12}C in the atmosphere today. (The assumption is made that this ratio has not changed throughout the years.)

This ratio decreases exponentially and has the same half-life as ^{14}C, which is 5730 years.

EXAMPLE 4

How old is a fossil whose $\frac{^{14}C}{^{12}C}$ ratio is 10 percent of that found in the atmosphere today?

Solution

Let $r(t)$ represent the ratio of ^{14}C to ^{12}C present after t years. Since $r(t)$ decreases exponentially,

$$r(t) = r_0e^{-kt}$$

156

To find k, we recall that $k = \dfrac{\ln 2}{T} = \dfrac{\ln 2}{5730}$.

$$r(t) = r_0 e^{-\left(\frac{\ln 2}{5730}\right)t}$$

$$\frac{r(t)}{r_0} = e^{-\left(\frac{\ln 2}{5730}\right)t}$$

Since $\dfrac{r(t)}{r_0} = 10\% = 0.1$, we have

$$0.1 = e^{-\left(\frac{\ln 2}{5730}\right)t}$$

$$\ln 0.1 = -\left(\frac{\ln 2}{5730}\right)t$$

$$t = \frac{-5730(\ln 0.1)}{\ln 2} \approx 19{,}034.6$$

The fossil is approximately 19,000 years old.

Continuous Compounding of Interest

If P dollars are invested in a bank account at an annual rate of interest r compounded n times per year, the amount of money A in the account after t years is

$$A = P\left(1 + \frac{r}{n}\right)^{nt}$$

Quarterly compounding, monthly compounding, and daily compounding use values of $n = 4$, 12, and 365, respectively. (Some banks use a 360-day business year, but there is virtually no difference in the interest between 360 and 365 days.)

If we let $n \to \infty$, we get what is called *continuous compounding of interest*, and the amount of money in the account after t years becomes

$$A = \lim_{n \to \infty}\left[P\left(1 + \frac{r}{n}\right)^{nt}\right]$$

$$= P\left[\lim_{n \to \infty}\left(1 + \frac{r}{n}\right)^{n}\right]^{t}$$

It can be shown that $\lim_{n\to\infty}\left(1+\dfrac{r}{n}\right)^{n}=e^{r}$, so the amount of money after t years compounded continuously is $A=Pe^{rt}$. The growth of money compounded continuously is exponential.

EXAMPLE 5

Compute the amount of money in the bank after 10 years when $1000 is compounded quarterly, monthly, daily, and continuously at an annual rate of 6 percent.

Solution

Quarterly :
$$A = 1000\left(1+\frac{0.06}{4}\right)^{40} = \$1814.02$$

Monthly :
$$A = 1000\left(1+\frac{0.06}{12}\right)^{120} = \$1819.40$$

Daily :
$$A = 1000\left(1+\frac{0.06}{365}\right)^{3650} = \$1822.03$$

Continuously : $A = 1000e^{0.6} = \$1822.12$

EXAMPLE 6

How long will it take money to double if it is compounded continuously at an annual rate of 5 percent?

Solution

The amount of money we start with is irrelevant. The important thing is that we end up with twice as much as we started with. If we start with P dollars, we must end up with $2P$ dollars.

$$A = Pe^{rt}$$
$$2P = Pe^{0.05\,t}$$
$$2 = e^{0.05\,t}$$

$$\ln 2 = 0.05t$$

$$t = \frac{\ln 2}{0.05} \approx 13.86 \text{ years}$$

EXAMPLE 7

How much money should Ariel invest in a bank account paying 8 percent annual interest compounded continuously if she wants to use the money to buy a $20,000 car in 4 years?

Solution

The equation $A = Pe^{rt}$ is equivalent to $P = \dfrac{A}{e^{rt}} = Ae^{-rt}$.

$$P = Ae^{-rt}$$

$$= 20{,}000e^{-(0.08)(4)}$$

$$= 20{,}000e^{-0.32}$$

$$= 20{,}000(0.726149)$$

$$= \$14{,}522.98$$

Additional Exponential Models

Exponential functions are prevalent in many problems in science, business, economics, medicine, and sociology. One important function, the *logistic function*, is often used to analyze population growth that is limited by natural environmental factors. The logistic function is also used to analyze the spread of epidemics and the propagation of rumors.

The general form of the logistic function is $P(t) = \dfrac{B}{1 + Ae^{-Bkt}}$ where A, B, and k are usually determined experimentally. Once these values are found, the logistic function can answer many questions concerning growth.

EXAMPLE 8

Environmentalists predict that in t years the deer population in a forest will be $P(t) = \dfrac{20}{1 + 4e^{-2t}}$ thousand.

159

(*a*) What is the current population?

(*b*) What will be the population at the end of each year for the first three years?

(*c*) What is the population growth rate after three years?

(*d*) When does the population growth rate begin to decline?

(*e*) What is the population limit of the deer in this forest?

(*f*) When will the deer population reach 80 percent of its limit?

Solution

The graph of the deer population is shown to the right.

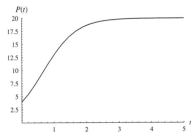

(*a*) $P(0) = 4$ thousand deer

(*b*) $P(1) = 12.98$ thousand deer
$P(2) = 18.63$ thousand deer
$P(3) = 19.80$ thousand deer

(*c*) The rate of population growth is given by $r(t) = P'(t)$.

$$P(t) = \frac{20}{1 + 4e^{-2t}} = 20(1 + 4e^{-2t})^{-1}$$

$$P'(t) = -20(1 + 4e^{-2t})^{-2}(-8e^{-2t})$$

$$= \frac{160e^{-2t}}{(1 + 4e^{-2t})^2}$$

After three years the population rate of change is

$P'(3) = \dfrac{160e^{-6}}{(1 + 4e^{-6})^2} \approx 0.389$. The rate of growth is 389 deer per year.

(*d*) The *rate* of population growth increases when $r'(t) > 0$ and decreases when $r'(t) < 0$. The population growth rate begins to decline when $r'(t) = P''(t) = 0$.

$$P''(t) = \frac{(1 + 4e^{-2t})^2 \dfrac{d}{dt}(160e^{-2t}) - (160e^{-2t})\dfrac{d}{dt}(1 + 4e^{-2t})^2}{(1 + 4e^{-2t})^4}$$

$$= \frac{(1 + 4e^{-2t})^2(-320e^{-2t}) - (160e^{-2t})(2)(1+4e^{-2t})(-8e^{-2t})}{(1 + 4e^{-2t})^4}$$

$$= \frac{-320e^{-2t}(1+4e^{-2t})[1+4e^{-2t}-8e^{-2t}]}{(1+4e^{-2t})^4}$$

$$= \frac{-320e^{-2t}(1-4e^{-2t})}{(1+4e^{-2t})^3}$$

$P''(t) = 0$ if and only if

$$1 - 4e^{-2t} = 0$$

$$1 = 4e^{-2t}$$

$$e^{2t} = 4$$

$$2t = \ln 4$$

$$t = \frac{1}{2}\ln 4 \approx 0.693 \text{ year}$$

(e) $P(t) = \dfrac{20}{1 + 4e^{-2t}}$. As $t \to \infty, e^{-2t} \to 0$ so $\displaystyle\lim_{t\to\infty} P(t) = $ 20 thousand deer.

(f) 80 percent of $20{,}000 = 16{,}000$ deer so we need to find t for which $P(t) = 16$.

$$P(t) = \frac{20}{1 + 4e^{-2t}}$$

$$16 = \frac{20}{1 + 4e^{-2t}}$$

$$16(1 + 4e^{-2t}) = 20$$

$$1 + 4e^{-2t} = \frac{5}{4}$$

$$4e^{-2t} = \frac{1}{4}$$

$$e^{-2t} = \frac{1}{16}$$

$$e^{2t} = 16$$

$$2t = \ln 16$$

$$t = \frac{1}{2}\ln 16 \approx 1.39 \text{ years}$$

EXAMPLE 9

According to Newton's law of cooling, the temperature of an object changes at a rate proportional to the difference in temperature between the object and the outside medium. If an object whose temperature is 70° Fahrenheit is placed in a medium whose temperature is 20° and is found to be 40° after 3 minutes, what will its temperature be after 6 minutes?

Solution

If $u(t)$ represents the temperature of the object at time t, $\dfrac{du}{dt}$ represents its rate of change. Newton's law of cooling may be written $\dfrac{du}{dt} = k(u - 20)$.

$$\frac{1}{u - 20} \frac{du}{dt} = k$$

$$\frac{d}{dt} \ln(u - 20) = k$$

$$\ln(u - 20) = kt + C$$

We can solve for C by observing that $u(0) = 70$

$$\ln(70 - 20) = k \cdot 0 + C$$

$$C = \ln 50$$

Next we determine $u(t)$.

$$\ln(u - 20) = kt + \ln 50$$

$$\ln(u - 20) - \ln 50 = kt$$

$$\ln\left(\frac{u - 20}{50}\right) = kt$$

$$\frac{u - 20}{50} = e^{kt}$$

$$u(t) = 20 + 50e^{kt}$$

To find k we use the given information $u(3) = 40$.

$$40 = 20 + 50e^{3k}$$

$$20 = 50e^{3k}$$

$$e^{3k} = \frac{2}{5}$$

$$3k = \ln\frac{2}{5}$$

$$k = \frac{1}{3}\ln\frac{2}{5}$$

The general solution becomes

$$u(t) = 20 + 50e^{(\frac{1}{3}\ln\frac{2}{5})t}$$

$$= 20 + 50(e^{\ln\frac{2}{5}})^{t/3}$$

$$= 20 + 50\left(\frac{2}{5}\right)^{t/3}$$

To find the temperature after 6 minutes, we compute $u(6)$.

$$u(6) = 20 + 50\left(\frac{2}{5}\right)^{2}$$

$$= 20 + 50\left(\frac{4}{25}\right)$$

$$= 28$$

The temperature after 6 minutes is $28°$ Fahrenheit.

Supplementary Problems

1. The growth rate of a bacteria culture is proportional to the number of bacteria present. If a population whose size is initially 100 bacteria doubles every 2 hours,

(a) How many bacteria will there be after 3 hours?

(b) How long will it take for the culture to grow to a size of 5000 bacteria?

2. One hour after a bacteria colony starts growing, a scientist determines that there are 9000 bacteria present. After another hour, there are 12,000 bacteria. How many bacteria were present initially?

3. A radioactive substance whose mass is 200 mg will decay to 180 mg after 12 years. Determine the half-life of this substance.

4. 10 mg of a radioactive substance with a half-life of 20 hours is injected into a patient's bloodstream. The patient returns to the medical facility after 24 hours and a technician determines that there are 2 mg of the substance in the patient's pancreas. How much of the substance is in the remainder of the patient's body?

5. An Egyptian papyrus is discovered and it is found that the ratio of ^{14}C to ^{12}C is 65 percent of the known ratio of ^{14}C to ^{12}C in the air today. The half-life of ^{14}C is 5730 years. How old is the papyrus?

6. How much money will Alexis have in the bank after 3 years if she invests $700 at 8 percent compounded continuously?

7. How long will it take money to triple if it is compounded continuously at a rate of 10 percent ?

8. Trevor would like to purchase an engagement ring that sells for $8000. How much should he put into a savings account today that pays 5 percent compounded continuously to have enough money to purchase the ring in 6 months?

9. An ecological study shows that a lake can support a maximum population of 5000 fish. The logistic function that governs the fish population is $P(t) = \dfrac{5000}{1 + 4e^{-0.4t}}$ where t is measured in months.

(a) How many fish were initially placed into the lake?

(b) How many fish are in the lake after 5 months?

(c) What is the population growth rate after 5 months?

(d) When does the population growth rate of the fish in the pond begin to decline?

(e) When will the number of fish in the pond be 70 percent of the pond's capacity?

10. A public health report states that t weeks after the outbreak of a new strain of flu, the number of people, in thousands, who will contract the disease is $Q(t) = \dfrac{10}{1 + 100e^{-1.5t}}$.

(a) How many people initially contracted the disease and how many people contracted the disease within the next two weeks?

(b) At what rate did people contract the disease after two weeks?

(c) When did the rate of infection begin to decline?

(d) If left untreated, how many people would eventually contract the flu?

11. On a day when the temperature is 30° Celsius, a cool drink is taken from a refrigerator whose temperature is 5°. If the temperature of the drink is 20° after 10 minutes, what will its temperature be after 20 minutes?

Solutions to Supplementary Problems

1. Let $y(t)$ represent the size of the population after t hours. Since the rate of growth of the bacteria is proportional to the number of bacteria present, $\dfrac{dy}{dt} = ky$ and it follows that $y = y_0 e^{kt}$. When $t = 0$, $y_0 = 100$ and the population function becomes $y(t) = 100e^{kt}$. Since the population doubles every 2 hours, $y = 200$ when $t = 2$. This allows us to determine k.

$$y = 100e^{kt}$$

$$200 = 100e^{2k}$$

$$2 = e^{2k}$$

$$2k = \ln 2$$

$$k = \frac{1}{2} \ln 2$$

We may now write the complete population function:

$$y(t) = 100e^{\left(\frac{1}{2} \ln 2\right)t}$$

$$= 100e^{\frac{t}{2} \ln 2}$$

(a) $y(3) = 100e^{\frac{3}{2} \ln 2} \approx 100(2.828) = 282.8$. There are 283 bacteria after 2 hours.

(b) We wish to determine the value of t for which $y(t) = 5000$.

$$100e^{\frac{t}{2}\ln 2} = 5000$$

$$e^{\frac{t}{2}\ln 2} = 50$$

$$\frac{t}{2}\ln 2 = \ln 50$$

$$\frac{t}{2} = \frac{\ln 50}{\ln 2}$$

$$t = \frac{2\ln 50}{\ln 2} \approx 11.29$$

It takes approximately 11.29 hours for the population to reach 5000.

2. Let $y(t)$ be the population of the colony t hours after the colony starts growing. Assuming the rate at which the colony grows is proportional to the size of the colony, we have $\dfrac{dy}{dt} = ky$. This leads to the solution $y = y_0 e^{kt}$. We wish to determine y_0, the value of y when $t = 0$. When $t = 1$, $y = 9000$ and when $t = 2$, $y = 12,000$. Substituting, we obtain

$$9000 = y_0 e^k$$

$$12,000 = y_0 e^{2k}$$

Dividing the second equation by the first, we obtain

$$\frac{12,000}{9000} = \frac{y_0 e^{2k}}{y_0 e^k}$$

$$\frac{4}{3} = e^k$$

$$k = \ln \frac{4}{3}$$

Since $9000 = y_0 e^k$, it follows that

$$9000 = y_0 e^{\ln \frac{4}{3}}$$

$$9000 = y_0 \left(\frac{4}{3}\right)$$

$$y_0 = 9000 \times \frac{3}{4} = 6750 \text{ bacteria}$$

3. The function representing the amount of the substance remaining after t years is $Q(t) = Q_0 e^{-kt}$. The initial amount, $Q_0 = Q(0) = 200$.

To determine the value of k, we substitute $Q(12) = 180$ into $Q(t) = 200e^{-kt}$.

$$Q(12) = 200e^{-12k}$$

$$180 = 200e^{-12k}$$

$$\frac{9}{10} = e^{-12k}$$

$$-12k = \ln \frac{9}{10}$$

$$k = -\frac{1}{12} \ln \frac{9}{10} = \frac{1}{12} \ln \frac{10}{9}$$

The function becomes $Q(t) = 200e^{-\left(\frac{1}{12} \ln \frac{10}{9}\right)t}$. To determine the half-life, we find the value of t for which $Q(t) = 100$, half the original mass.

$$Q(t) = 200e^{-\left(\frac{1}{12} \ln \frac{10}{9}\right)t}$$

$$100 = 200e^{-\left(\frac{1}{12} \ln \frac{10}{9}\right)t}$$

$$\frac{1}{2} = e^{-\left(\frac{1}{12} \ln \frac{10}{9}\right)t}$$

$$-\left(\frac{1}{12} \ln \frac{10}{9}\right)t = \ln \frac{1}{2}$$

$$t = \frac{-12 \ln \frac{1}{2}}{\ln \frac{10}{9}} \approx 78.95 \text{ years}$$

4. The function that governs the decay of the radioactive substance is $Q(t) = Q_0 e^{-kt}$ where $Q_0 = 10$ and $k = \frac{\ln 2}{T} = \frac{\ln 2}{20}$.

$$Q(t) = 10e^{-\left(\frac{\ln 2}{20}\right)t}$$

After 24 hours, the amount of the substance within the patient's body is

$$Q(24) = 10e^{-\left(\frac{\ln 2}{20}\right)24}$$

$$= 10e^{-\frac{24\ln 2}{20}}$$

$$= 10e^{-1.2\ln 2}$$

$$\approx 4.35 \text{ mg}$$

Since 2 mg are found in the pancreas, 2.35 mg (4.35 mg $-$ 2 mg) are in the remainder of the patient's body.

5. The ratio $r(t)$ of ^{14}C to ^{12}C present in the papyrus is $r(t) = r_0 e^{-kt}$. Since the half-life is $T = 5730$ years, $k = \dfrac{\ln 2}{T} = \dfrac{\ln 2}{5730}$.

$$\frac{r(t)}{r_0} = e^{-kt}$$

$$0.65 = e^{-\left(\frac{\ln 2}{5730}\right)t}$$

$$-\left(\frac{\ln 2}{5730}\right)t = \ln 0.65$$

$$t = -(\ln 0.65)\left(\frac{5730}{\ln 2}\right)$$

$$t \approx 3561.1$$

The papyrus is about 3561 years old.

6. The amount of money P dollars will be worth in t years if compounded continuously at rate r is

$$A = Pe^{rt}$$

In this problem, $P = 700$, $r = 0.08$, and $t = 3$.

$$A = 700e^{(0.08)(3)}$$

$$= 700e^{0.24}$$

$$= 700(1.271249)$$

$$= \$889.87$$

7. After t years P dollars will be worth an amount $A = Pe^{rt}$. We would like to determine the value of t when $A = 3P$.

$$A = Pe^{rt}$$

$$3P = Pe^{0.1t}$$

$$3 = e^{0.1t}$$

$$0.1t = \ln 3$$

$$t = \frac{\ln 3}{0.1} \approx \frac{1.0986}{0.1} = 10.986$$

It will take almost 11 years for the money to triple.

8. $A = Pe^{rt}$. In this problem, $A = 8000$ and we wish to find P. The value of $r = 0.05$ and $t = \frac{1}{2}$ year.

$$A = Pe^{rt}$$

$$8000 = Pe^{(0.05)\left(\frac{1}{2}\right)}$$

$$8000 = Pe^{0.025}$$

$$P = 8000e^{-0.025}$$

$$= 8000 \times 0.9753$$

$$\approx \$7802.48$$

9. $P(t) = \dfrac{5000}{1 + 4e^{-0.4t}}$.

(a) The number of fish initially placed into the lake is the population at time $t = 0$.

$$P(0) = \frac{5000}{1 + 4e^{-(0.4)(0)}} = \frac{5000}{1 + 4} = 1000 \text{ fish}$$

(b) The population of fish after 5 months is $P(5)$.

$$P(5) = \frac{5000}{1 + 4e^{-(0.4)(5)}} = \frac{5000}{1 + 4e^{-2}}$$

$$= \frac{5000}{1 + 4(0.135335)} \approx 3244 \text{ fish}$$

(c) The population growth rate is the derivative of the population function $P(t)$.

$$P(t) = \frac{5000}{1 + 4e^{-0.4t}}$$

$$= 5000(1 + 4e^{-0.4t})^{-1}$$

$$P'(t) = -5000(1 + 4e^{-0.4t})^{-2}(-1.6e^{-0.4t})$$

$$= \frac{8000e^{-0.4t}}{(1 + 4e^{-0.4t})^2}$$

The growth rate after 5 months is $P'(5) = \dfrac{8000e^{-2}}{(1 + 4e^{-2})^2} \approx 456$ fish per month.

(d) The population growth rate will begin to decline when $P''(t)$ turns from positive to negative. Since $P''(t)$ is a continuous function, we must determine where $P''(t) = 0$.

$$P'(t) = \frac{8000e^{-0.4t}}{(1 + 4e^{-0.4t})^2}$$

$$P''(t) = \frac{(1 + 4e^{-0.4t})^2 \dfrac{d}{dt}(8000e^{-0.4t}) - (8000e^{-0.4t})\dfrac{d}{dt}(1 + 4e^{-0.4t})^2}{(1 + 4e^{-0.4t})^4}$$

$$= \frac{(1 + 4e^{-0.4t})^2(-3200e^{-0.4t}) - (8000e^{-0.4t})(2)(1 + 4e^{-0.4t})(-1.6e^{-0.4t})}{(1 + 4e^{-0.4t})^4}$$

$$= \frac{-3200e^{-0.4t}(1 + 4e^{-0.4t})[(1 + 4e^{-0.4t}) - 8e^{-0.4t}]}{(1 + 4e^{-0.4t})^4}$$

$$= \frac{-3200e^{-0.4t}[(1 + 4e^{-0.4t}) - 8e^{-0.4t}]}{(1 + 4e^{-0.4t})^3}$$

$$0 = \frac{-3200e^{-0.4t}[1 - 4e^{-0.4t}]}{(1 + 4e^{-0.4t})^3}$$

The only way $P''(t)$ can be 0 is if $1 - 4e^{-0.4t} = 0$.

$$1 - 4e^{-0.4t} = 0$$

$$1 = 4e^{-0.4t}$$

$$e^{-0.4t} = \frac{1}{4}$$

$$-0.4t = \ln \frac{1}{4}$$

$$0.4t = \ln 4$$

$$t = \frac{\ln 4}{0.4} \approx 3.47 \text{ months}$$

(e) The fish population will be at 70 percent of the pond's capacity of 5000 when $P(t) = 3500$.

$$3500 = \frac{5000}{1 + 4e^{-0.4t}}$$

$$3500(1 + 4e^{-0.4t}) = 5000$$

$$1 + 4e^{-0.4t} = \frac{10}{7}$$

$$4e^{-0.4t} = \frac{3}{7}$$

$$e^{-0.4t} = \frac{3}{28}$$

$$-0.4t = \ln \frac{3}{28}$$

$$0.4t = \ln \frac{28}{3}$$

$$t = \frac{\ln \frac{28}{3}}{0.4} \approx 5.58 \text{ months.}$$

10. (a) The number of people who initially contracted the disease is

$$Q(0) = \frac{10}{1 + 100e^0} = \frac{10}{101} \approx 0.099 \text{ (in thousands)}$$

99 people initially contracted the disease.

(b) The infection rate is $Q'(t)$.

$$Q(t) = \frac{10}{1 + 100e^{-1.5t}}$$

$$= 10(1 + 100e^{-1.5t})^{-1}$$

$$Q'(t) = -10(1 + 100e^{-1.5t})^{-2}(-150e^{-1.5t})$$

$$= \frac{1500e^{-1.5t}}{(1 + 100e^{-1.5t})^2}$$

After 2 weeks, $Q'(2) = \dfrac{1500e^{-3}}{(1 + 100e^{-3})^2} \approx 2.089$. The infection rate is 2089 people per week.

(c) The rate of infection increases when $Q''(t) > 0$ and decreases when $Q''(t) < 0$. The infection rate begins to decline when $Q''(t) = 0$.

$$Q'(t) = \frac{1500e^{-1.5t}}{(1 + 100e^{-1.5t})^2}$$

$$Q''(t) = \frac{(1 + 100e^{-1.5t})^2\frac{d}{dt}(1500e^{-1.5t}) - (1500e^{-1.5t})\frac{d}{dt}(1 + 100e^{-1.5t})^2}{(1 + 100e^{-1.5t})^4}$$

$$= \frac{(1 + 100e^{-1.5t})^2(-2250e^{-1.5t}) - (1500e^{-1.5t})(2)(1 + 100e^{-1.5t})(-150e^{-1.5t})}{(1 + 100e^{-1.5t})^4}$$

$$= \frac{-2250(1 + 100e^{-1.5t})e^{-1.5t}[(1 + 100e^{-1.5t}) - 200e^{-1.5t}]}{(1 + 100e^{-1.5t})^4}$$

$$= \frac{-2250(1 + 100e^{-1.5t})e^{-1.5t}(1 - 100e^{-1.5t})}{(1 + 100e^{-1.5t})^4}$$

$$0 = \frac{-2250e^{-1.5t}(1 - 100e^{-1.5t})}{(1 + 100e^{-1.5t})^3}$$

Since $2250e^{-1.5t} \neq 0$, it follows that

$$1 - 100e^{-1.5t} = 0$$

$$1 = 100e^{-1.5t}$$

$$\frac{1}{100} = e^{-1.5t}$$

$$-1.5t = \ln\frac{1}{100}$$

$$1.5t = \ln 100$$

$$t = \frac{\ln 100}{1.5} \approx 3.07$$

The rate of infection starts to decline 3.07 weeks after the outbreak begins.

(d) $\displaystyle\lim_{t\to\infty} Q(t) = \lim_{t\to\infty} \frac{10}{1 + 100e^{-1.5t}} = 10$

10,000 people would contract the disease if no medical treatment were received.

11. Let $u(t)$ represent the temperature of the drink t minutes after it is taken out of the refrigerator. Since the temperature changes at a rate proportional to the difference in temperature between the object and the outside medium, $\dfrac{du}{dt} = k(u - 30)$.

$$\frac{1}{u - 30}\frac{du}{dt} = k$$

$$\frac{d}{dt}\ln(u - 30) = k$$

> The antiderivative of $\dfrac{1}{u - 30}$ is $\ln|u - 30|$. Since $u < 30$, this reduces to $\ln(30 - u)$.

$$\ln(30 - u) = kt + C$$

The initial temperature, $u(0) = 5$ so $\ln 25 = C$.

$$\ln(30 - u) = kt + \ln 25$$

$$\ln(30 - u) - \ln 25 = kt$$

$$\ln\left(\frac{30 - u}{25}\right) = kt$$

$$\frac{30 - u}{25} = e^{kt}$$

$$30 - u = 25e^{kt}$$

$$u(t) = 30 - 25e^{kt}$$

Since the drink's temperature after 10 minutes is $20°$, $u(10) = 20$.

$$u(10) = 30 - 25e^{10k}$$

$$20 = 30 - 25e^{10k}$$

$$-10 = -25e^{10k}$$

$$\frac{2}{5} = e^{10k}$$

$$10k = \ln \frac{2}{5}$$

$$k = \frac{1}{10} \ln \frac{2}{5}$$

The temperature function is $u(t) = 30 - e^{\left(\frac{1}{10} \ln \frac{2}{5}\right)t}$. After 20 minutes the temperature will be

$$u(20) = 30 - 25e^{2\ln \frac{2}{5}}$$

$$= 30 - 25(e^{\ln \frac{2}{5}})^2$$

$$= 30 - 25 \left(\frac{2}{5}\right)^2$$

$$= 30 - 25 \left(\frac{4}{25}\right)$$

$$= 26 \text{ degrees}$$

Chapter 7

Problems Involving Integrals

Area Problems

If $y = f(x)$ is *nonnegative* between a and b, the area of the region
bounded by its graph and the x axis between the vertical lines
$x = a$ and $x = b$ is the value of the definite integral

$$A = \int_a^b f(x)\,dx$$

A simple mnemonic device for remembering this formula is
to think of a rectangle, infinitesimally thin, whose height
is $y = f(x)$ and whose width is dx. The area of this imaginary rectangle would be $y\,dx$. If we "add up" all such rectangular areas between a and b by integrating, we obtain
$A = \int_a^b y\,dx$.

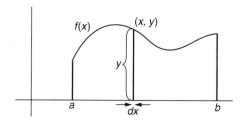

EXAMPLE I

Find the area of the region bounded by
$y = x^3 - 3x^2 + 2x + 1$, the x axis, and the vertical lines $x = 0$
and $x = 2$.

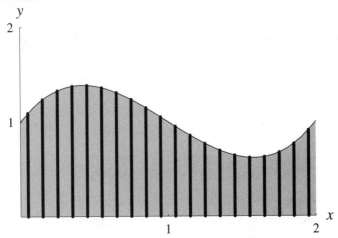

The diagram shows the function $y = x^3 - 3x^2 + 2x + 1$ drawn with about 20 "imaginary" vertical rectangles of height y and thickness dx. If we imagine an *infinite number* of such rectangles extending from $x = 0$ to $x = 2$, each *infinitesimally thin*, the rectangles will "color in" the required area. Since integration is a summation process, $\int_0^2 y\, dx$ will yield the exact area.

$$\int_0^2 y\, dx = \int_0^2 (x^3 - 3x^2 + 2x + 1)\, dx$$

$$= \left[\frac{x^4}{4} - x^3 + x^2 + x \right]_0^2$$

$$= (4 - 8 + 4 + 2) - (0)$$

$$= 2$$

In Example 1 we were given the interval of integration. Often this interval is determined by the x intercepts of the graph. These intercepts can be found by setting $f(x) = 0$ and solving for x. (It is always advisable to sketch a graph of the region whose area is to be found.)

EXAMPLE 2

Find the area of the region above the x axis bounded by the function $y = 4x - x^2 - 3$.

176

Solution

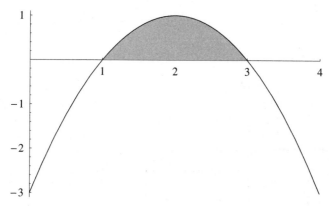

The x intercepts are determined by setting $y = 0$ and solving for x.

$$y = 4x - x^2 - 3$$
$$0 = 4x - x^2 - 3$$
$$x^2 - 4x + 3 = 0$$
$$(x - 1)(x - 3) = 0$$
$$x = 1 \qquad x = 3$$

The area may then be easily computed by integrating from 1 to 3.

$$A = \int_1^3 y \, dx$$

$$= \int_1^3 (4x - x^2 - 3) \, dx$$

$$= \left[2x^2 - \frac{x^3}{3} - 3x \right]_1^3$$

$$= \left(2(3)^2 - \frac{3^3}{3} - 3(3) \right) - \left(2(1)^2 - \frac{1^3}{3} - 3(1) \right)$$

$$= 0 - \left(-\frac{4}{3} \right)$$

$$= \frac{4}{3}$$

If $f(x)$ is negative over all or part of $[a, b]$, the integral $\int_a^b f(x)\,dx$ will *not* give the desired area; the area must be determined by computing $\int_a^b |f(x)|\,dx$. Since the Fundamental Theorem of Calculus cannot be conveniently applied to a function involving an absolute value, one must first determine where the graph crosses the x axis, break up the interval into subintervals determined by these points, integrate separately in each subinterval, and add the absolute values of the integrals. The next example illustrates this procedure.

EXAMPLE 3

Find the area of the region bounded by $y = x^2 - 5x + 6$, the x axis, and the vertical lines $x = 0$ and $x = 4$.

Solution

First we draw a sketch of the area to be determined.

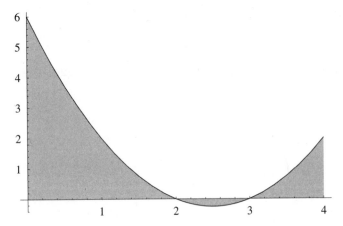

Next, we determine where the graph crosses the x axis.

$$y = x^2 - 5x + 6$$
$$0 = x^2 - 5x + 6$$
$$0 = (x - 2)(x - 3)$$
$$x = 2 \qquad x = 3$$

We integrate separately on the three intervals [0, 2], [2, 3], and [3, 4].

$$I_1 = \int_0^2 (x^2 - 5x + 6)\, dx = \left[\frac{x^3}{3} - \frac{5x^2}{2} + 6x \right]_0^2$$

$$= \left(\frac{8}{3} - \frac{20}{2} + 12 \right) - (0) = \frac{14}{3}$$

$$I_2 = \int_2^3 (x^2 - 5x + 6)\, dx = \left[\frac{x^3}{3} - \frac{5x^2}{2} + 6x \right]_2^3$$

$$= \left(9 - \frac{45}{2} + 18 \right) - \left(\frac{8}{3} - \frac{20}{2} + 12 \right)$$

$$= \frac{9}{2} - \frac{14}{3} = -\frac{1}{6}$$

$$I_3 = \int_3^4 (x^2 - 5x + 6)\, dx = \left[\frac{x^3}{3} - \frac{5x^2}{2} + 6x \right]_3^4$$

$$= \left(\frac{64}{3} - 40 + 24 \right) - \left(9 - \frac{45}{2} + 18 \right)$$

$$= \frac{16}{3} - \frac{9}{2} = \frac{5}{6}$$

To obtain the required area, we add the absolute values of I_1, I_2, and I_3.

$$\text{Area} = |I_1| + |I_2| + |I_3| = \frac{14}{3} + \frac{1}{6} + \frac{5}{6} = \frac{17}{3}$$

To determine the area bounded by two curves, $y = f(x)$ and $y = g(x)$, we must first determine their points of intersection. This may be done by solving the equation $f(x) = g(x)$. If the curves intersect at only two locations, say $x = a$ and $x = b$, and $f(x)$ lies above $g(x)$, i.e., $f(x) \geq g(x)$ for $x \varepsilon$ [a, b], the area will be

$$A = \int_a^b [f(x) - g(x)]\, dx$$

If the curves intersect at more than two locations, the area must be computed by subdividing the interval, integrating separately in each subinterval, and adding the absolute values of the integrals, in a manner similar to Example 3.

To extend our mnemonic device to areas bounded by two curves, consider an infinitesimally thin rectangle of width dx extending from $y_1 = g(x)$ to $y_2 = f(x)$. Its height is $y_2 - y_1$ and its area is $(y_2 - y_1)dx$. The area of the region, obtained by integrating (adding), becomes $\int_a^b (y_2 - y_1)\, dx$.

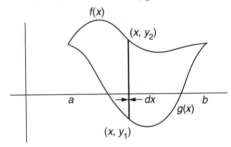

EXAMPLE 4

Determine the area of the region bounded by the parabola $y = 9 - x^2$ and the line $x + y = 7$.

Solution

The parabola is represented by the function $y_2 = f(x) = 9 - x^2$. To determine $g(x)$ we solve the line's equation for y:

$$x + y = 7$$

$$y = 7 - x$$

$$y_1 = g(x) = 7 - x$$

We will need the points of intersection of these two curves. This is accomplished by solving the equation $f(x) = g(x)$ for x.

$$9 - x^2 = 7 - x$$

$$0 = x^2 - x - 2$$

$$0 = (x + 1)(x - 2)$$

$$x = -1 \qquad x = 2$$

It is clear from a diagram that $f(x) \geq g(x)$ for $x \, \varepsilon \, [-1, 2]$.

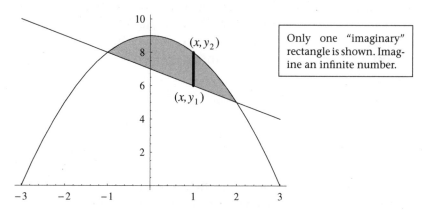

Only one "imaginary" rectangle is shown. Imagine an infinite number.

We are now ready to compute the area of the region bounded by the curves.

$$A = \int_a^b (y_2 - y_1) \, dx$$

$$= \int_{-1}^2 [f(x) - g(x)] \, dx$$

$$= \int_{-1}^2 [9 - x^2 - (7 - x)] \, dx$$

$$= \int_{-1}^2 [2 - x^2 + x] \, dx$$

$$= \left[2x - \frac{x^3}{3} + \frac{x^2}{2} \right]_{-1}^2$$

$$= \left(4 - \frac{8}{3} + 2 \right) - \left(-2 + \frac{1}{3} + \frac{1}{2} \right)$$

$$= \frac{10}{3} - \left(-\frac{7}{6} \right)$$

$$= \frac{9}{2}$$

Occasionally, it is more convenient to compute an area by evaluating an integral with respect to y rather than with respect to x. If the region is described as the intersection of the graphs $x = f(y)$ and $x = g(y)$, the area may be represented as an integral whose variable of integration is y.

$$A = \int_a^b [f(y) - g(y)]\, dy$$

It is assumed that a and b are the y coordinates of the points of intersection of the two graphs and $f(y) \geq g(y)$ for $y \, \varepsilon \, [a, b]$. In this type of problem our imaginary rectangles lie parallel to the x axis and extend, left to right, from $x_1 = g(y)$ to $x_2 = f(y)$.

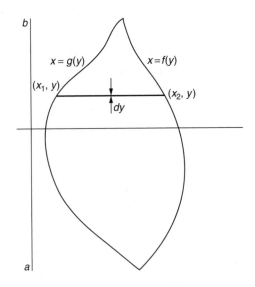

EXAMPLE 5

Find the area of the region bounded by the parabola $x = y^2$ and the line $y = x - 2$.

Solution

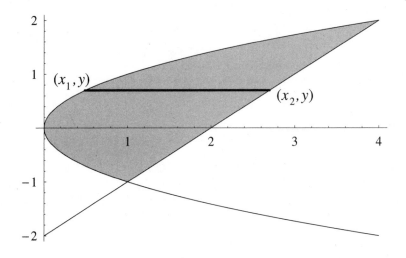

The equation $y = x - 2$ is equivalent to $x = y + 2$. Since the line lies to the right of the parabola within the region under consideration, we let $f(y) = y + 2$ and $g(y) = y^2$. (This guarantees that $f(y) - g(y)$ is nonnegative.) Their intersection points are computed by solving the equation $g(y) = f(y)$ for y.

$$y^2 = y + 2$$

$$y^2 - y - 2 = 0$$

$$(y + 1)(y - 2) = 0$$

$$y = -1 \qquad y = 2$$

$$A = \int_a^b (x_2 - x_1)\, dy$$

$$= \int_a^b [f(y) - g(y)]\,dy$$

$$= \int_{-1}^2 [(y+2) - y^2]\,dy$$

$$= \left[\frac{y^2}{2} + 2y - \frac{y^3}{3} \right]_{-1}^2$$

$$= \left(2 + 4 - \frac{8}{3} \right) - \left(\frac{1}{2} - 2 + \frac{1}{3} \right)$$

$$= \frac{10}{3} - \left(-\frac{7}{6} \right)$$

$$= \frac{9}{2}$$

Volumes of Solids of Revolution

If the region bounded by the function $y = f(x)$ and the x axis, between $x = a$ and $x = b$ is revolved about the x axis, the resulting three-dimensional figure is known as a *solid of revolution*. Its cross-sectional area is circular, and its volume may be computed by evaluating the integral

$$V = \pi \int_a^b [f(x)]^2\,dx$$

$$\text{or} \quad V = \pi \int_a^b y^2\,dx$$

A mnemonic device for remembering this formula is to think of the solid being "sliced" into infinitesimally thin disks of radius y and thickness dx. The volume of a typical disk is $\pi(\text{radius})^2(\text{thickness}) = \pi y^2\,dx$ and the sum of the volumes is $\pi \int_a^b y^2\,dx$. (Since π is a constant, it may be taken outside the integral.) This method is sometimes known as the *disk method*.

184

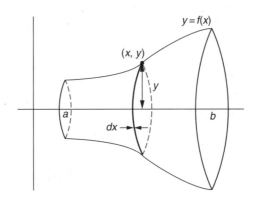

EXAMPLE 6

Find the volume of the solid of revolution obtained by revolving the region bounded by $y = x - x^2$ and the x axis about the x axis.

Solution

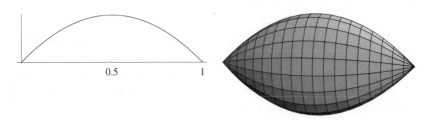

The graph intersects the x axis when $y = 0$.

$$y = x - x^2$$
$$0 = x - x^2$$
$$0 = x(1 - x)$$
$$x = 0 \qquad x = 1$$

The volume of each "imaginary" circular disk is $\pi y^2 \, dx$ and the volume of the region is obtained by integrating, with respect to x, from 0 to 1.

$$V = \pi \int_0^1 y^2 \, dx$$

$$= \pi \int_0^1 (x - x^2)^2 \, dx$$

$$= \pi \int_0^1 (x^2 - 2x^3 + x^4) \, dx$$

$$= \pi \left[\frac{x^3}{3} - \frac{2x^4}{4} + \frac{x^5}{5} \right]_0^1$$

$$= \pi \left[\frac{1}{3} - \frac{2}{4} + \frac{1}{5} - 0 \right]$$

$$= \frac{\pi}{30}$$

If the region bounded by two curves is revolved about the x axis, the resulting solid of revolution will be hollow. Its cross section will be in the shape of a washer, i.e., the area between two concentric circles. The following method of computing volume is named the *washer method*.

If the inner radius is y_1 and the outer radius is y_2, and we think of the thickness of the washer as dx, the volume of the washer is $V_{\text{outer} \atop \text{disk}} - V_{\text{inner} \atop \text{disk}} = \pi y_2^2 \, dx - \pi y_1^2 \, dx = \pi (y_2^2 - y_1^2) \, dx$.

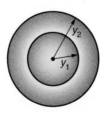

The volume of the solid of revolution, expressed as an integral, becomes

$$V = \pi \int_a^b \left(y_2^2 - y_1^2\right) dx$$

EXAMPLE 7

Find the volume obtained if the region bounded by $y = x^2$ and $y = 2x$ is rotated about the x axis.

Solution

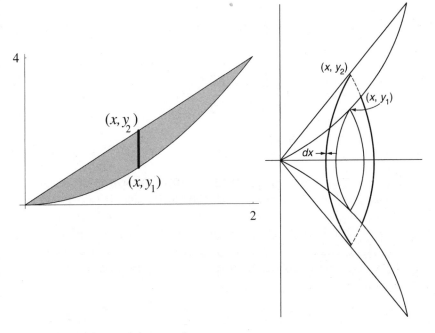

First we must determine the points of intersection of the two curves.

$$x^2 = 2x$$
$$x^2 - 2x = 0$$
$$x(x - 2) = 0$$
$$x = 0 \qquad x = 2$$

When the region is rotated, the outer radius of the washer, y_2, is determined by the line and the inner radius, y_1, by the parabola.

$$V = \pi \int_a^b (y_2^2 - y_1^2)\, dx$$

$$= \pi \int_0^2 [(2x)^2 - (x^2)^2]\, dx$$

$$= \pi \int_0^2 [4x^2 - x^4]\, dx$$

$$= \pi \left[\frac{4x^3}{3} - \frac{x^5}{5} \right]_0^2$$

$$= \pi \left[\frac{32}{3} - \frac{32}{5} - 0 \right]$$

$$= \frac{64}{15}\pi$$

Another method for computing volumes of solids of revolution, the *shell method*, uses a different approach for constructing an integral representing volume. Consider a thin-wall cylindrical shell having inner and outer radii r_1 and r_2, respectively, where $r_1 \approx r_2$, and height h. (Imagine a soup can with its top and bottom cut out. The thickness of the wall of the can is $r_2 - r_1$.)

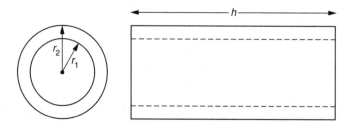

The volume of the shell is the difference between two cylindrical volumes.

$$V_{shell} = V_{outer \atop cylinder} - V_{inner \atop cylinder}$$

$$= \pi r_2^2 h - \pi r_1^2 h$$

$$= \pi \left(r_2^2 - r_1^2 \right) h$$

$$= \pi (r_2 + r_1)(r_2 - r_1) h$$

$$= 2\pi \left(\frac{r_2 + r_1}{2} \right) h(r_2 - r_1)$$

If we let $r_{av} = \dfrac{r_2 + r_1}{2}$ represent the average radius and $\Delta r = r_2 - r_1$ represent the shell wall thickness, we may write

$$V_{shell} = 2\pi r_{av} \, h \, \Delta r$$

As $\Delta r \to 0$, and the number of shells within the solid $\to \infty$, the sum of their volumes will approach the volume of the solid of revolution.

As a mnemonic device we may represent the average radius by r, the length of the shell by h, and the (infinitesimal) shell wall thickness by dr. The volume of a typical shell may be thought of as $2\pi r h \, dr$ and the total volume is

$$\boxed{V = 2\pi \int_a^b r h \, dr}$$

In a given problem, dr will be replaced by either dx or dy, depending upon the axis of rotation (dx if rotated about the y axis and dy if rotated about the x axis). In either case, the height h and the radius r must be expressed in terms of the variable of integration. The limits of integration must correspond to the variable of integration as well.

EXAMPLE 8

Find the volume of the solid of revolution formed by rotating the region bounded by the parabola $y = x^2$ and the lines $y = 0$ and $x = 2$ about the x axis.

Solution

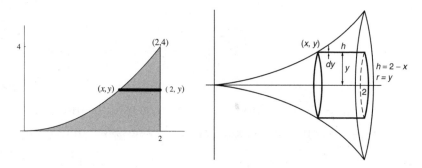

If (x, y) represents an arbitrary point on the graph $y = x^2$, the length of the generated shell is $h = 2 - x$, the radius $r = y$, and the thickness of the shell is dy. The volume of a typical shell is $2\pi y(2 - x)\,dy$ and the total volume of the solid is obtained by integration. Since the volume of the shell involves dy, integration will be with respect to y. Since $y = x^2$, $y = 0$ when $x = 0$ and $y = 4$ when $x = 2$. Therefore,

$$V = 2\pi \int_0^4 y(2 - x)\,dy$$

The variable x must be expressed in terms of y before the integration can be performed. Since $y = x^2$, $x = \sqrt{y}$.

$$V = 2\pi \int_0^4 y(2 - \sqrt{y})\,dy$$

$$= 2\pi \int_0^4 (2y - y^{3/2})\,dy$$

190

$$= 2\pi \left[y^2 - \frac{2}{5}y^{5/2} \right]_0^4$$

$$= 2\pi \left(16 - \frac{2}{5}4^{5/2} - 0 \right)$$

$$= 2\pi \left(16 - \frac{64}{5} \right)$$

$$= 2\pi \left(\frac{16}{5} \right)$$

$$= \frac{32}{5}\pi$$

The nature of the shell method makes it well suited for finding volumes of "hollow" solids.

EXAMPLE 9

Find the volume obtained if the region bounded by $y = x^2$ and $y = 2x$ is rotated about the x axis. (This problem was solved previously using the washer method. See Example 7 for comparison.)

Solution

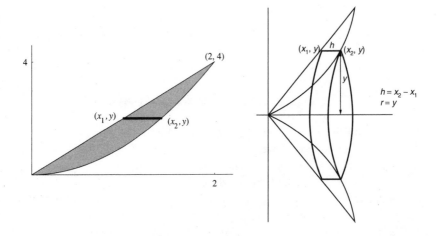

The length of each shell $h = x_2 - x_1$ and the radius $r = y$. The thickness of each shell is dy. Therefore, the volume of a typical shell is $2\pi(x_2 - x_1)y\,dy$ and the total volume is

$$V = 2\pi \int_a^b (x_2 - x_1)y\,dy$$

The variable of integration is y so both x_1 and x_2 must be expressed in terms of y. The limits of integration must also correspond to y.

Since the equation of the parabola is $y = x^2$, $x_2 = \sqrt{y}$ and the line's equation $y = 2x$ gives $x_1 = \dfrac{y}{2}$. The points of intersection are $(0, 0)$ and $(2, 4)$. The volume is therefore

$$V = 2\pi \int_0^4 \left(\sqrt{y} - \frac{y}{2}\right)y\,dy$$

$$= 2\pi \int_0^4 \left(y^{3/2} - \frac{1}{2}y^2\right)dy$$

$$= 2\pi \left[\frac{2}{5}y^{5/2} - \frac{1}{6}y^3\right]_0^4$$

$$= 2\pi \left(\frac{64}{5} - \frac{64}{6} - 0\right)$$

$$= \frac{64}{15}\pi$$

Supplementary Problems

1. Compute the area of the region bounded by the curve
    $y = 8 - x^2 - 2x$ and the x axis.
2. Determine the area of the region bounded by the curve
    $y = x^3 - 4x^2 + 3x$ and the x axis, $0 \le x \le 3$.
3. Find the area of the region bounded by the curve $y = x^3$ and the line
    $y = 8$ using (a) vertical rectangles and (b) horizontal rectangles.
4. Determine the area of the region bounded by the curves
    $y = x^4 - x^2$ and $y = x^2 - 1$.

192

5. Find the area of the region bounded by the curves $4x - y^2 = 0$ and $y = 2x - 4$.
6. Find the area of the region bounded by the parabola $y = x^2$, the tangent line to the parabola at the point $(2, 4)$, and the x axis.
7. Derive a formula for the volume of a sphere of radius r by rotating the semicircle $y = \sqrt{r^2 - x^2}$ about the x axis.
8. Compute the volume of the solid obtained by rotating the region bounded by $y = x^2$, $y = 8 - x^2$, and the y axis about the x axis.
9. A hole of radius 2 is drilled through the axis of a sphere of radius 3. Compute the volume of the remaining solid.

Solutions to Supplementary Problems

1. We begin by sketching the region.

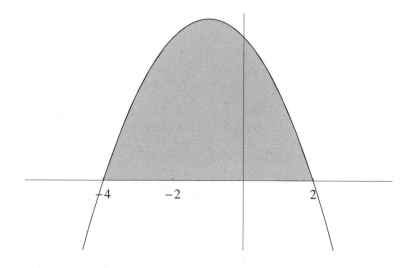

Next we must determine where the parabola crosses the x axis.

$$y = 0$$
$$8 - x^2 - 2x = 0$$
$$x^2 + 2x - 8 = 0$$
$$(x + 4)(x - 2) = 0$$
$$x = -4 \qquad x = 2$$

We integrate to get the area.

$$A = \int_{-4}^{2} (8 - x^2 - 2x)\, dx$$

$$= \left[8x - \frac{x^3}{3} - x^2 \right]_{-4}^{2}$$

$$= \left(16 - \frac{8}{3} - 4 \right) - \left(-32 + \frac{64}{3} - 16 \right)$$

$$= \frac{28}{3} - \left(-\frac{80}{3} \right)$$

$$= \frac{108}{3}$$

$$= 36$$

2.

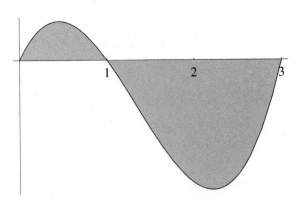

There appear to be three x intercepts. We first compute their exact locations.

$$y = 0$$

$$x^3 - 4x^2 + 3x = 0$$

$$x(x^2 - 4x + 3) = 0$$

$$x(x - 1)(x - 3) = 0$$

$$x = 0 \qquad x = 1 \qquad x = 3$$

Since the graph falls below the x axis, we must integrate separately over two intervals.

$$I_1 = \int_0^1 (x^3 - 4x^2 + 3x)\,dx \qquad\qquad I_2 = \int_1^3 (x^3 - 4x^2 + 3x)\,dx$$

$$= \left[\frac{x^4}{4} - \frac{4x^3}{3} + \frac{3x^2}{2}\right]_0^1 \qquad\qquad = \left[\frac{x^4}{4} - \frac{4x^3}{3} + \frac{3x^2}{2}\right]_1^3$$

$$= \left(\frac{1}{4} - \frac{4}{3} + \frac{3}{2}\right) - 0 \qquad\qquad = \left(\frac{81}{4} - \frac{108}{3} + \frac{27}{2}\right)$$

$$= \frac{5}{12} \qquad\qquad\qquad\qquad\qquad\qquad\quad - \left(\frac{1}{4} - \frac{4}{3} + \frac{3}{2}\right)$$

$$\qquad\qquad\qquad\qquad\qquad\qquad\qquad = -\frac{9}{4} - \frac{5}{12}$$

$$\qquad\qquad\qquad\qquad\qquad\qquad\qquad = -\frac{8}{3}$$

I_2 is negative since the curve falls below the x axis between $x = 1$ and $x = 2$. The total area is computed by adding the absolute values of the integrals.

$$A = |I_1| + |I_2| = \frac{5}{12} + \frac{8}{3} = \frac{37}{12}$$

3. (a)

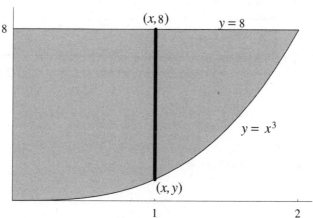

Think of each vertical rectangle as having (mnemonically) length $8 - y$ and width dx. Its area is $(8 - y)\,dx$. The total area of the region is

$$A = \int_0^2 (8 - y)\,dx$$

$$= \int_0^2 (8 - x^3)\,dx$$

$$= \left[8x - \frac{x^4}{4} \right]_0^2$$

$$= (16 - 4) - 0$$

$$= 12$$

(b)

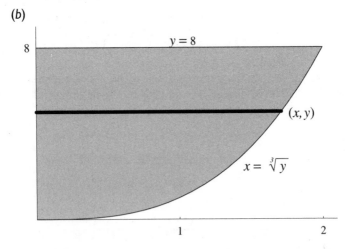

Using horizontal rectangles, the length of each rectangle is x and the width is dy. We integrate with respect to y from 0 to 8.

$$A = \int_0^8 x\,dy$$

$y = x^3$ is equivalent to $x = \sqrt[3]{y}$

$$= \int_0^8 \sqrt[3]{y}\,dy$$

$$= \int_0^8 y^{1/3}\,dy$$

$$= \left[\frac{3}{4}y^{4/3}\right]_0^8$$

$$= \frac{3}{4}(8)^{4/3} - 0$$

$$= 12$$

4.

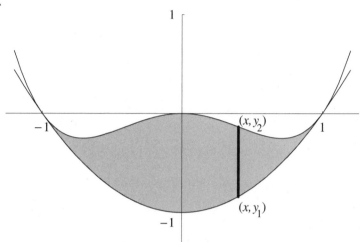

Let $y_1 = x^2 - 1$ and $y_2 = x^4 - x^2$. We determine the intersection points of the two graphs by setting $y_2 = y_1$ and solving the resulting equation.

$$x^4 - x^2 = x^2 - 1$$

$$x^4 - 2x^2 + 1 = 0$$

$$(x^2 - 1)^2 = 0$$

$$x^2 - 1 = 0$$

$$x = \pm 1$$

Using vertical rectangles "coloring in" the region from -1 to 1, the height of each rectangle is $y_2 - y_1$ and the width is dx. The area is computed by integration. For convenience, we take advantage of symmetry, integrating from 0 to 1 and doubling the value of the integral. (Note that even though both curves fall below the x axis,

$y_2 - y_1$ is still positive throughout the region since y_1 is more negative than y_2. This guarantees that the integral will represent the area.)

$$A = \int_{-1}^{1} (y_2 - y_1)\, dx$$

$$= 2 \int_{0}^{1} (y_2 - y_1)\, dx$$

$$= 2 \int_{0}^{1} [(x^4 - x^2) - (x^2 - 1)]\, dx$$

$$= 2 \int_{0}^{1} (x^4 - 2x^2 + 1)\, dx$$

$$= 2 \left[\frac{x^5}{5} - \frac{2x^3}{3} + x \right]_{0}^{1}$$

$$= 2 \left(\frac{1}{5} - \frac{2}{3} + 1 - 0 \right)$$

$$= 2 \left(\frac{8}{15} \right)$$

$$= \frac{16}{15}$$

5.

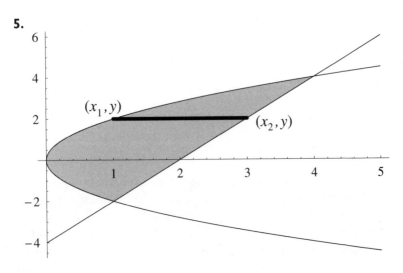

(x_1, y)

(x_2, y)

We first find the intersection points by solving each equation for x.

$$4x - y^2 = 0 \qquad y = 2x - 4$$

$$4x = y^2 \qquad y + 4 = 2x$$

$$x = \frac{y^2}{4} \qquad x = \frac{y+4}{2}$$

Now we set $\dfrac{y^2}{4} = \dfrac{y+4}{2}$ and solve for y.

$$2y^2 = 4y + 16$$

$$2y^2 - 4y - 16 = 0$$

$$y^2 - 2y - 8 = 0$$

$$(y - 4)(y + 2) = 0$$

$$y = -2 \qquad y = 4$$

The best way to proceed in this problem is to use horizontal rectangles. The length of each rectangle may be thought of as $x_2 - x_1$ and the width dy

$$A = \int_{-2}^{4} (x_2 - x_1)\, dy$$

$$= \int_{-2}^{4} \left[\frac{y+4}{2} - \frac{y^2}{4} \right] dy$$

$$= \int_{-2}^{4} \left[\frac{1}{2}y + 2 - \frac{1}{4}y^2 \right] dy$$

$$= \left[\frac{1}{4}y^2 + 2y - \frac{1}{12}y^3 \right]_{-2}^{4}$$

$$= \left(4 + 8 - \frac{64}{12} \right) - \left(1 - 4 + \frac{8}{12} \right)$$

$$= \frac{20}{3} - \left(-\frac{7}{3} \right)$$

$$= 9$$

6. Let $f(x) = x^2$. The slope of the tangent line at $(2, 4)$ is $m = f'(2)$.

$$f(x) = x^2$$

$$f'(x) = 2x$$

$$f'(2) = 4$$

The equation of the tangent line can be constructed using the standard equation for a line:

$$y - y_1 = m(x - x_1)$$

$$y - 4 = 4(x - 2)$$

$$y - 4 = 4x - 8$$

$$y = 4x - 4$$

Once we sketch the curve and the tangent line, it becomes clear that horizontal rectangles are best to use.

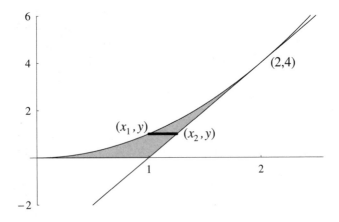

Solving for x in terms of y, the equation $y = x^2$ becomes $x = \sqrt{y}$ and $y = 4x - 4$ becomes $x = \dfrac{y + 4}{4}$.

$$A = \int_0^4 (x_2 - x_1)\, dy$$

$$= \int_0^4 \left[\frac{y + 4}{4} - \sqrt{y} \right] dy$$

$$= \int_0^4 \left[\frac{1}{4}y + 1 - y^{1/2} \right] dy$$

$$= \left[\frac{1}{8}y^2 + y - \frac{2}{3}y^{3/2} \right]_0^4$$

$$= 2 + 4 - \frac{16}{3} - 0$$

$$= \frac{2}{3}$$

7.

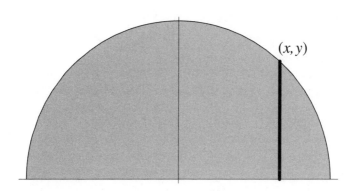

(x, y)

If the vertical rectangle shown is rotated about the x axis,
a disk of radius y and thickness dx is generated. The volume
of a typical disk is $\pi y^2 \, dx$ and the total volume of the solid of
revolution is

$$V = \pi \int_{-r}^r y^2 \, dx$$

> We take advantage of symmetry by integrating from 0 to r and doubling the integral.

$$= 2\pi \int_0^r \left(\sqrt{r^2 - x^2} \right)^2 dx$$

$$= 2\pi \int_0^r (r^2 - x^2) \, dx$$

$$= 2\pi \left[r^2 x - \frac{x^3}{3} \right]_0^r$$

$$= 2\pi \left[\left(r^3 - \frac{r^3}{3} \right) - 0 \right]$$

$$= 2\pi \left(\frac{2}{3} r^3 \right)$$

$$= \frac{4}{3} \pi r^3$$

8.

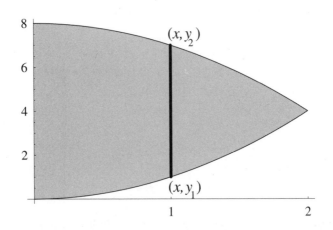

The x coordinate of the intersection point of the two curves is easily calculated:

$$x^2 = 8 - x^2$$

$$2x^2 = 8$$

$$x^2 = 4$$

$$x = 2$$

Using the washer method, the vertical rectangle shown above generates a washer of inner radius y_1, outer radius y_2, and thickness dx. The volume of a typical washer is $(\pi y_2^2 - \pi y_1^2)\, dx = \pi(y_2^2 - y_1^2)\, dx$.

The total volume

$$V = \pi \int_0^2 \left(y_2^2 - y_1^2\right) dx$$

$$= \pi \int_0^2 \left[(8 - x^2)^2 - (x^2)^2\right] dx$$

$$= \pi \int_0^2 \left[64 - 16x^2 + x^4 - x^4\right] dx$$

$$= \pi \int_0^2 \left[64 - 16x^2\right] dx$$

$$= \pi \left[64x - \frac{16x^3}{3}\right]_0^2$$

$$= \pi \left[128 - \frac{128}{3} - 0\right]$$

$$= \frac{256\pi}{3}$$

9. At first, this appears to be a simple problem: Why not simply subtract the volume of the cylinder from the volume of the sphere? The figure below shows why this is not a valid approach, as part of the sphere is eliminated when the hole is drilled.

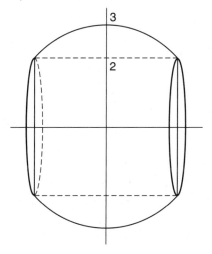

The sphere is generated by rotating the upper half of the circle $x^2 + y^2 = 9$ about the x axis. We solve this problem using the shell method, using shells of radius y and length $2x$.

$$V = 2\pi \int_a^b hr\, dr$$

$$= 2\pi \int_2^3 2xy\, dy$$

Since the variable of integration is y, we must replace x in terms of y. Since $x^2 + y^2 = 9$, it follows that in the first quadrant $x = \sqrt{9 - y^2}$. Hence

$$V = 2\pi \int_2^3 2y\sqrt{9 - y^2}\, dy$$

We evaluate this integral by making the substitution $u = 9 - y^2$. It follows that $du = -2y\, dy$. We change the limits of integration by observing that $u = 5$ when $y = 2$ and $u = 0$ when $y = 3$.

$$V = -2\pi \int_5^0 \sqrt{u}\, du$$

$$= 2\pi \int_0^5 u^{1/2}\, du$$

$$= 2\pi \left[\frac{2}{3} u^{3/2} \right]_0^5$$

$$= \frac{4}{3}\pi (5^{3/2} - 0)$$

$$= \frac{20\pi \sqrt{5}}{3}$$

Chapter 8

Application to Business and Economics

Rates of Change in Business

Many quantities in the business world are constantly changing. For example, your salary may increase if you stay with the same company for many years or your debt may decrease if you pay back your student loan.

It is useful to know *how fast* a quantity is changing. After all, an employee whose salary changes by $10,000 over a 2-year time period is doing better than an employee whose salary changes by the same amount over 5 years.

The derivative with respect to time measures how fast a function is changing. This is known as the instantaneous rate of change with respect to time. (See Chapter 2 for a discussion of rates of change.)

EXAMPLE I

t years after it was built, the property tax T on a small home was $T(t) = 15t^2 + 35t + 2500$ dollars. How fast did the property tax increase 2 years after the home was built?

Solution

$$T'(t) = 30t + 35$$

$$T'(2) = 95$$

The tax increased at the rate of $95 per year.

EXAMPLE 2

A publisher estimates that t months after he introduces a new magazine, the circulation will be
$C(t) = 150t^2 + 400t + 7000$ copies. If this prediction is correct, how fast will circulation increase 6 months after the magazine is introduced?

Solution

$$C'(t) = 300t + 400$$

$$C'(6) = 300(6) + 400 = 2200 \text{ copies per month}$$

Sometimes it is useful to understand how a quantity's change is related to variables other than time. For example, a manufacturer's profit may change with the number of items produced and sold or his production cost may change with the availability of raw materials. In general, the derivative $y'(x)$ or dy/dx measures the rate of change of the variable y with respect to x.

EXAMPLE 3

The demand q for a certain commodity expressed as a function of its selling price p is $q(p) = 200p - 100p^2 + 5000$ units. At what rate is q changing with respect to p when the selling price is \$5? Is demand increasing or decreasing at this price?

Solution

$$q'(p) = 200 - 200p$$

$$q'(5) = -800$$

The rate of change when $p = 5$ is -800 units per dollar. Since this number is negative, demand is decreasing.

EXAMPLE 4

A computer manufacturer's total cost in dollars when q units are produced is given by the function
$C(q) = 500q + 5000e^{-q/10}$. At what rate is his cost changing when 20 units are produced?

206

Solution

$$C'(q) = 500 - 500e^{-\frac{q}{10}}$$

$$C'(20) = 500 - 500e^{-2}$$

$$= 500 - 67.67$$

$$= 432.33$$

His cost is increasing at the rate of $432.33 per unit.

Marginal Analysis in Economics

In economics, the *marginal cost* (*MC*) of producing an item is the rate at which its cost changes with respect to the number of items produced. Thus if $C(x)$ is the cost of producing x items, the marginal cost is $C'(x)$. Similarly, if $R(x)$ and $P(x)$ represent the revenue and profit, respectively, in selling a quantity of x units, then $R'(x)$ represents marginal revenue (*MR*) and $P'(x)$ marginal profit (*MP*).

EXAMPLE 5

It costs $0.05x^2 + 6x + 100$ dollars to produce x pounds of soap. Because of quantity discounts, each pound sells for $12 - 0.15x$ dollars. Compute the marginal cost, marginal revenue, and marginal profit when $x = 10$.

Solution

$$C(x) = 0.05x^2 + 6x + 100$$

$$MC(x) = C'(x) = 0.1x + 6$$

$$MC(10) = \$7.00$$

$$R(x) = \text{(price per pound)(number of pounds sold)}$$

$$= (12 - 0.15x)(x)$$

$$= 12x - 0.15x^2$$

$$MR(x) = R'(x) = 12 - 0.3x$$

$$MR(10) = \$9.00$$

Since $P(x) = R(x) - C(x)$,

$$MP(x) = MR(x) - MC(x)$$
$$MP(10) = MR(10) - MC(10)$$
$$= 9.00 - 7.00$$
$$= \$2.00$$

By definition of the derivative of $C(x)$,

$MC(x) = C'(x)$

$$= \lim_{h \to 0} \frac{C(x+h) - C(x)}{h}$$

$$\approx \frac{C(x+h) - C(x)}{h} \qquad \text{if } h \text{ is small in comparison to } x.$$

If $h = 1$

$$MC(x) \approx C(x+1) - C(x)$$

Thus the marginal cost approximates the additional cost incurred in producing *one* additional item. Similarly,

$$MR(x) \approx R(x+1) - R(x)$$

and

$$MP(x) \approx P(x+1) - P(x)$$

EXAMPLE 6

The cost of manufacturing x baseballs is $C(x) = 0.05x^2 + 0.5x + 50$. How much will it cost to produce the 101st baseball? Find the exact value and compare with the approximate value using marginal cost.

208

Solution

Exact solution

The cost of producing 101 baseballs is

$$C(101) = 0.05(101)^2 + 0.5(101) + 50 = \$610.55$$

The cost of producing 100 baseballs is

$$C(100) = 0.05(100)^2 + 0.5(100) + 50 = \$600.00$$

The cost of producing the 101st baseball is

$$C(101) - C(100) = 610.55 - 600.00 = \$10.55$$

Approximation using marginal cost

$$MC(x) = C'(x) = 0.1x + 0.5$$

$$MC(100) = C'(100) = 0.1(100) + 0.5 = \$10.50$$

The derivative offers an excellent approximation.

EXAMPLE 7

A manufacturer estimates that the cost of producing x units of a product is $C(x) = 0.1x^2 + 3x + 100$ dollars and that he will be able to sell x units when the price is $p(x) = 25 - 0.05x$ dollars per unit.

(a) Determine the marginal cost function and use it to approximate the cost of producing the 21st unit. Compare this with the actual cost.

(b) Determine the marginal revenue function for this product. Use it to approximate the additional revenue from the sale of the 21st unit and compare with the actual value.

Solution

(a)
$$MC(x) = C'(x) = 0.2x + 3$$

$$MC(20) = \$7.00$$

The actual cost of producing the 21st unit =
$C(21) - C(20) = \$207.10 - \$200.00 = \$7.10$.
(b) Since x units will be sold when the price is $p(x)$ dollars,

$$R(x) = xp(x)$$
$$= x(25 - 0.05x)$$
$$= 25x - 0.05x^2$$
$$R'(x) = 25 - 0.1x$$
$$R'(20) = \$23.00$$

The actual revenue derived from the 21st unit =
$R(21) - R(20) = \$502.95 - \$480.00 = \$22.95$.

Related Rates

As we saw in Chapter 3, the rate at which one quantity changes is often related to the rate of change of other quantities. The following steps outline the procedure for solving a related rates business problem.

Step 1
Label all variables with an appropriate symbol. (In business problems, diagrams are often inappropriate. However, all variables should be clearly labeled for reference.)

Step 2
Determine which rates are given and which rate you need to find. Write them down for future reference.

Step 3
Determine an equation (or several equations) relating the variables defined in step 1.

Step 4
Differentiate the equation(s) in step 3 with respect to time.

EXAMPLE 8

The cost $C(x)$, in thousands of dollars, of a full-page advertisement in a magazine is related to its monthly circulation by the function $C(x) = 5\sqrt{x^2 - 900}$. We assume $x \geq 30$, where x is the circulation in thousands of copies sold. If the circulation is increasing at the rate of 3000 copies per month, how fast is the cost of advertising increasing when 50,000 copies are being sold?

Solution

Step 1

$$x = \text{circulation (thousands of copies)}$$
$$C = \text{cost (thousands of dollars)}$$

Step 2

Given: $\dfrac{dx}{dt} = 3$ Find: $\dfrac{dC}{dt}$ when $x = 50$

Step 3

$$C = 5\sqrt{x^2 - 900}$$
$$= 5(x^2 - 900)^{1/2}$$

Step 4

$$\frac{dC}{dt} = \frac{dC}{dx} \cdot \frac{dx}{dt}$$
$$\frac{dC}{dt} = \frac{5}{2}(x^2 - 900)^{-1/2}(2x)\frac{dx}{dt}$$
$$= \frac{5x}{\sqrt{x^2 - 900}}\frac{dx}{dt}$$

Step 5

When $x = 50$, $\dfrac{dC}{dt} = \dfrac{250}{\sqrt{2500 - 900}} \cdot 3 = \dfrac{750}{40} = 18.75$.

The cost of advertising is increasing at the rate of \$18,750 per month.

EXAMPLE 9

The wholesale price p of string beans, in dollars per bushel, and the daily supply x, in thousands of bushels, are related by the equation

$$px + 6x + 7p = 5950$$

If the supply is decreasing at the rate of 2000 bushels per day, at what rate is the daily bushel price changing when 100,000 bushels are available? Is the price increasing or decreasing?

Solution

Step 1

x = supply of string beans (thousands of bushels)

p = price per bushel (dollars)

Step 2

Given: $\dfrac{dx}{dt} = -2$

> dx/dt is negative, since supply is decreasing.

Find: $\dfrac{dp}{dt}$ when $x = 100$

Step 3

$$px + 6x + 7p = 5950$$

Step 4

$p\dfrac{dx}{dt} + x\dfrac{dp}{dt} + 6\dfrac{dx}{dt} + 7\dfrac{dp}{dt} = 0$ ← We use the product rule to find the derivative of px.

Step 5

We know the values of x and dx/dt and we are looking for dp/dt. To find p when $x = 100$ we go back to the original equation.

$$px + 6x + 7p = 5950$$
$$100p + 600 + 7p = 5950$$
$$107p = 5350$$
$$p = 50$$

Now we can solve for dp/dt:

$$50(-2) + 100\frac{dp}{dt} + 6(-2) + 7\frac{dp}{dt} = 0$$

$$107\frac{dp}{dt} - 112 = 0$$

$$\frac{dp}{dt} = \frac{112}{107} \approx 1.0467$$

The price is *increasing* by approximately $1.05 per bushel per day.

EXAMPLE 10

The demand x for milk (quarts), selling for p dollars per quart at a supermarket is determined by the equation $px + 1200p - 6000 = 0$. If the price is increasing at the rate of 3 cents per week, at what rate is demand changing when the price is $1.25 per quart?

Solution

Step 1

$$x = \text{demand for milk (quarts)}$$
$$p = \text{price per quart (in dollars)}$$

Step 2

Given: $\dfrac{dp}{dt} = 0.03$ Find: $\dfrac{dx}{dt}$ when $p = 1.25$

Step 3

$$px + 1200p - 6000 = 0$$

213

Step 4

$$p\frac{dx}{dt} + x\frac{dp}{dt} + 1200\frac{dp}{dt} = 0$$

Step 5

When $p = 1.25$, we get, from step 3,

$$1.25x + 1200(1.25) - 6000 = 0$$

$$1.25x + 1500 - 6000 = 0$$

$$1.25x = 4500$$

$$x = 3600$$

From step 4,

$$1.25\frac{dx}{dt} + 3600(0.03) + 1200(0.03) = 0$$

$$1.25\frac{dx}{dt} + 108 + 36 = 0$$

$$1.25\frac{dx}{dt} = -144$$

$$\frac{dx}{dt} = -115.2$$

The demand for milk *decreases* at the rate of 115.2 quarts per week.

Optimization

Optimization problems are very important in business. Whether we are trying to maximize our profit or minimize our cost, knowing how to determine optimal values is extremely useful.

The procedures illustrated in Chapter 4 for finding the maximum or minimum value of a function extend in a very natural way to business problems. We list the main steps for review.

214

Step 1

Draw a diagram (if appropriate). Label all quantities, known and unknown, which will be used in the problem.

Step 2

Write an equation representing the quantity to be maximized or minimized.

Step 3

Use any constraints or relationships between the variables to eliminate all but one independent variable. This gives a *function* representing the quantity to be maximized or minimized.

Step 4

Find all critical numbers. A critical number for f is a number x for which either $f'(x) = 0$ or $f'(x)$ does not exist. (In business problems it is *extremely rare* that $f'(x)$ will fail to exist.)

Step 5

(optional) Use an appropriate test to confirm your absolute maximum or minimum value (closed interval method, first or second derivative tests—see Chapter 4). This step may be omitted if you obtain only one critical number and you are confident that the problem has a solution.

EXAMPLE 11

The wholesale price of a designer shirt is $25. A retail store has determined that if they sell the shirt for $40, consumers will purchase 55 shirts per month. The manager of the men's department knows that for each dollar decrease in price, 5 more shirts will be sold each month. What selling price will yield the greatest monthly profit for the store?

Solution

Step 1

In this type of problem it is convenient to let x represent the *decrease* in the price per shirt. The selling price is thus $40 - x$ dollars.

Step 2
The total profit to the store is
$P(x) = $ (profit per shirt) $\times$ (number of shirts sold).

Step 3
Since the cost of the shirt is \$25, the store's profit per shirt is $(40 - x) - 25 = 15 - x$. The number of shirts sold at this price is $55 + 5x$ since 5 more shirts are sold for each dollar decrease in price.

$$P(x) = (15 - x)(55 + 5x)$$
$$= 825 + 20x - 5x^2$$

Step 4
$$P'(x) = 20 - 10x$$
$$0 = 20 - 10x$$
$$10x = 20$$
$$x = 2$$

Step 5
(optional) $P''(x) = -10$ for all x. Since the second derivative is negative, the critical number represents a relative maximum. Since there is only one relative extremum, the absolute maximum profit occurs when $x = 2$.
The optimal selling price is \$40 − \$2 = \$38.

Inventory Control

When a company orders spare parts or raw materials, two specific costs are incurred.

(a) The company must pay an ordering fee to cover handling and transportation costs.
(b) The company must pay a storage fee to cover the cost of keeping the items on hand until needed. These costs are known as storage or holding costs.

If each shipment is large, fewer shipments will be needed and consequently the ordering fees will be small. However, holding costs will be higher. If many small shipments are made,

216

holding costs will be small, but the total ordering fees will be large. We will use calculus to determine the lot size x of each shipment that minimizes the total cost.

The cost incurred is $C(x) = H(x) + O(x)$, where $H(x)$ represents the total holding cost and $O(x)$ is the total ordering cost.

Assuming that the demand for the product is uniform throughout the year, the *average* yearly holding cost to store a lot of size x is the same as if $x/2$ items were stored for the entire year. Therefore

$$H(x) = \text{(annual storage cost per item)} \left(\frac{x}{2} \right)$$

If q items are ordered in lots of size x, then the total number of shipments necessary will be q/x. Consequently,

$$O(x) = \text{(cost per order)(number of orders)}$$

$$= \text{(cost per order)} \left(\frac{q}{x} \right)$$

The total cost is then

$$C(x) = H(x) + O(x)$$

$$= \text{(annual storage cost per item)} \left(\frac{x}{2} \right)$$

$$+ \text{(cost per order)} \left(\frac{q}{x} \right)$$

Once the function $C(x)$ is constructed we apply maximum-minimum theory to determine the value of x that minimizes total cost.

EXAMPLE 12

A home improvement company expects to sell 180 kitchen sinks during the year. There is a $60 ordering fee for each shipment of sinks and it costs $6 to hold a sink for a year. How many sinks should the company order in each shipment to minimize total cost?

Solution

Let x = number of sinks ordered in each shipment.

$$C(x) = H(x) + O(x)$$

$$= 6\left(\frac{x}{2}\right) + 60\left(\frac{180}{x}\right)$$

$$= 3x + 10,800x^{-1} \qquad x > 0$$

$$C'(x) = 3 - 10,800x^{-2}$$

$$0 = 3 - \frac{10,800}{x^2}$$

$$\frac{10,800}{x^2} = 3$$

$$3x^2 = 10,800$$

$$x^2 = 3600$$

$$x = 60$$

Since $C''(x) = 21,600x^{-3} = \dfrac{21,600}{x^3}$, it is clear that $C''(60) > 0$. Hence $x = 60$ corresponds to a relative minimum and, since it is the only relative extremum for positive x, it represents the absolute minimum. (This is typical for inventory problems and this analysis may be omitted, if desired.)

Conclusion: The company should order sinks in lots of 60 to minimize total cost.

Note: You may have noticed that the actual cost of the sinks was not considered in the previous example. The cost is the same no matter what each lot size is and has no bearing on the solution. Mathematically this cost, obtained by multiplying the cost of each sink by 180, is constant and will be zero when differentiated. This is typical for inventory control problems.

EXAMPLE 13

A tire dealer buys 4000 tires a year from a local distributor. Each tire costs $75, the ordering fee is $30 per shipment, and

218

the storage cost is $24 per tire per year. How many tires should be ordered in each shipment in order to minimize the total cost?

Solution

Let x = size of each shipment. In this problem $C(x) = H(x) + O(x)$. The price per tire ($75) has no bearing on the solution (see note above). Assuming that the demand for the product is uniform throughout the year, it follows that

$$C(x) = 24\left(\frac{x}{2}\right) + 30\left(\frac{4000}{x}\right)$$

$$= 12x + 120{,}000x^{-1}$$

$$C'(x) = 12 - 120{,}000x^{-2}$$

$$0 = 12 - \frac{120{,}000}{x^2}$$

$$\frac{120{,}000}{x^2} = 12$$

$$12x^2 = 120{,}000$$

$$x^2 = 10{,}000$$

$$x = 100$$

In order to minimize cost, the tires should be ordered in 40 shipments of 100 tires each.

Supplementary Problems

1. If a company invests x thousand dollars in advertising, the demand for its product will be $D(x) = 2000x^2 + 900x + 60$ items. Find the rate of change in demand with respect to advertising dollars when $1500 is spent on advertising.

2. A family's demand x for gasoline at a selling price p is given by the function

$$x = 2000 - 100p - 0.05p^2$$

where x is measured in gallons and p is in dollars. At what rate is the demand changing when the selling price is $1.25 and dropping at the rate of 15 cents per month?

3. A yacht manufacturer finds that his profit in dollars for manufacturing and selling x yachts is given by the function $p(x) = (x^2 + 2x)^2$. If he can produce 4 yachts per month, at what rate is his profit increasing at the end of 6 months?

4. A manufacturer's total monthly revenue when x units are produced and sold is $R(x) = 300x + 0.075x^2$.

   (a) Use marginal analysis to estimate the additional revenue generated by the manufacture and sale of the 51st unit.

   (b) Compute the actual revenue generated by the manufacture and sale of the 51st unit.

5. The cost of manufacturing x units of a commodity is given by the function $C(x) = 50x + 400$. x units are sold when the price per unit is $500 - 2x$ dollars. Use marginal analysis to approximate the profit or loss incurred in manufacturing and selling the 100th unit. Compare this with the exact value.

6. When the price of a certain commodity is p dollars per unit, a manufacturer will supply x thousand units where $x^2 + 2x\sqrt{p} - p = 25$. If the price is increasing at the rate of $1 per week, how fast is the supply changing when the price is $100 per unit?

7. A small shop sells teddy bears for $28 each. The daily cost to produce x bears is determined by the function

$$C(x) = x^3 - 6x^2 + 13x + 15$$

Find the number of bears that should be produced and sold to maximize daily profit. What is the maximum profit?

8. A toll road averages 300,000 cars a day when the toll is $2.00 per car. A study has shown that for each 10-cent increase in the toll, 10,000 fewer cars will use the road each day. What toll will maximize the revenue?

9. A company makes and sells cameras at a price of $60 each. Its daily cost function is $C(x) = 40 + 4x - 1.6x^2 + 0.1x^3$ where x is the number of cameras manufactured and sold in a day. If the company can manufacture no more than 30 cameras per day, what level of production will yield the maximum profit?

10. A publisher plans to sell 200,000 copies of a textbook in a year. If it costs $3750 to set up a printing, $3 to print a book, and $600 to store 1000 books for a year, what size printing runs will minimize the publisher's cost?

220

Solutions to Supplementary Problems

1. In this problem x represents the company's advertising investment (thousands of dollars) and D represents the demand for the company's product (thousands of items). The rate at which demand is changing with respect to advertising dollars is $D'(x)$.

$$D(x) = 2000x^2 + 900x + 60$$

$$D'(x) = 4000x + 900$$

$$D'(1.5) = 4000(1.5) + 900 \qquad \boxed{x = 1.5 \text{ corresponds to } \$1500}$$

$$= 6900$$

   Demand increases at the rate of 6900 items per $1000 spent on advertising.

2. Let x = demand for gasoline $\qquad x = 2000 - 100\,p - .05\,p^2$
   p = selling price

   Given: $\dfrac{dp}{dt} = -0.15$ \qquad Find: $\dfrac{dx}{dt}$ when $p = 1.25$

   $$\frac{dx}{dt} = \frac{dx}{dp} \cdot \frac{dp}{dt}$$

   $$= (-100 - 0.1\,p)\frac{dp}{dt}$$

   When $p = 1.25$, $\quad \dfrac{dx}{dt} = (-100 - 0.125)(-0.15)$

   $$= 15.01875$$

   The family's demand for gasoline increases at the rate of 15.02 gallons per month.

3. Let x = number of yachts produced
   p = profit

   Given: $\dfrac{dx}{dt} = 4$ \qquad Find: $\dfrac{dp}{dt}$ after 6 months

$$p(x) = (x^2 + 2x)^2$$

$$\frac{dp}{dt} = \frac{dp}{dx} \cdot \frac{dx}{dt}$$

$$= 2(x^2 + 2x)(2x + 2)\frac{dx}{dt}$$

The number of yachts produced in 6 months $= 4 \cdot 6 = 24$

When $x = 24$, $\quad \dfrac{dp}{dt} = 2(24^2 + 48)(48 + 2)(4)$

$$= 2(624)(50)(4)$$

$$= 249,600 \text{ dollars per month}$$

4. (a) $R(x) = 300x + 0.075x^2$ 　(b) $R(51) = 300(51) + 0.075(51)^2$

$$= 15,495.08$$

$$R'(x) = 300 + 0.15x \qquad\qquad R(50) = 300(50) + 0.075(50)^2$$

$$= 15,187.50$$

$$R'(50) = 300 + 0.15(50) \qquad\qquad R(51) - R(50) = \$307.58$$

$$= \$307.50$$

5. Let $R(x)$, $C(x)$, and $P(x)$ represent the revenue, cost, and profit, respectively, in producing x items. Then $P(x) = R(x) - C(x)$

$$R(x) = (\text{price per unit sold})(\text{number of units sold})$$

$$= (500 - 2x)x$$

$$= 500x - 2x^2$$

$$P(x) = R(x) - C(x)$$

$$= 500x - 2x^2 - (50x + 400)$$

$$= 450x - 2x^2 - 400$$

$$P'(x) = 450 - 4x$$

$$P'(99) = \$54$$

The profit realized from the sale of the 100th unit is approximately $54. The exact profit $= P(100) - P(99) = 24{,}600 - 24{,}548 = \$52$.

6. Let $x =$ supply (thousands of units)

$p =$ price (dollars) per unit

Given: $\dfrac{dp}{dt} = 1$ Find: $\dfrac{dx}{dt}$ when $p = 100$

$$x^2 + 2x\sqrt{p} - p = 25$$

$$x^2 + 2xp^{1/2} - p = 25$$

$$2x\frac{dx}{dt} + 2\left[x\left(\frac{1}{2}p^{-1/2}\frac{dp}{dt}\right) + (p^{1/2})\frac{dx}{dt}\right] - \frac{dp}{dt} = 0$$

$$2x\frac{dx}{dt} + \frac{x}{\sqrt{p}}\frac{dp}{dt} + 2\sqrt{p}\frac{dx}{dt} - \frac{dp}{dt} = 0$$

We know $\dfrac{dp}{dt}$ and we know p at the instant in question. We need to determine the corresponding value of x.

$$x^2 + 2x\sqrt{p} - p = 25$$

When $p = 100$, $x^2 + 2x\sqrt{100} - 100 = 25$

$$x^2 + 20x - 100 = 25$$

$$x^2 + 20x - 125 = 0$$

$$(x + 25)(x - 5) = 0$$

$$x = 5 \qquad \text{(The value } x = -25 \text{ is discarded.)}$$

We substitute $x = 5$, $p = 100$, $\dfrac{dp}{dt} = 1$ and solve for $\dfrac{dx}{dt}$:

$$2(5)\frac{dx}{dt} + \frac{5}{\sqrt{100}}(1) + 2\sqrt{100}\frac{dx}{dt} - 1 = 0$$

$$10\frac{dx}{dt} + \frac{1}{2} + 20\frac{dx}{dt} - 1 = 0$$

$$30\frac{dx}{dt} = \frac{1}{2}$$

$$\frac{dx}{dt} = \frac{1}{60}$$

The supply increases at the rate of $\frac{1}{60}$ thousand (approximately 16.67) units per week.

7. If x bears are sold at \$28 each, the revenue derived from the sale is $28x$. We determine the profit function by subtracting cost from revenue.

$$P(x) = R(x) - C(x)$$
$$= 28x - (x^3 - 6x^2 + 13x + 15)$$
$$= 15x - x^3 + 6x^2 - 15$$

We proceed to find the critical value(s).

$$P'(x) = 15 - 3x^2 + 12x$$
$$0 = 15 - 3x^2 + 12x$$
$$0 = 5 - x^2 + 4x$$
$$x^2 - 4x - 5 = 0$$
$$(x - 5)(x + 1) = 0$$
$$x - 5 = 0, \ x + 1 = 0$$
$$x = 5 \qquad x = -1 \qquad \qquad (x = -1 \text{ is discarded.})$$

The maximum daily profit is $P(5) = \$85$.

(optional) To confirm that this is the number of teddy bears that maximizes profit, we use the second derivative test.

$$P''(x) = -6x + 12$$
$$P''(5) = -18$$

Since $P''(5) < 0$, the value $x = 5$ is a relative maximum. Since there is only one relative extremum for $x > 0$, $x = 5$ corresponds to the absolute maximum profit of \$85.

224

8. For convenience, we will let n represent the number of cars in units of 1000 and t, the toll, in dollars. If x represents the number of dimes to be charged in excess of $2.00, the toll will be $t = 2.00 + 0.10x$. Since the number of cars will decrease by 10,000 for each unit increment in x, the daily number of cars using the road will be $n = 300 - 10x$ thousand. The total revenue

$$R(x) = n \cdot t$$

$$= (300 - 10x)(2.00 + 0.10x)$$

$$= 600 + 10x - x^2$$

$$R'(x) = 10 - 2x$$

$$0 = 10 - 2x$$

$$x = 5$$

The toll should be increased by 50 cents (5×10 cents) to $2.50.

9. The profit function $P(x) = R(x) - C(x)$. Since the company sells the cameras at $60 each, $R(x) = 60x$. It follows that

$$P(x) = 60x - (40 + 4x - 1.6x^2 + 0.1x^3)$$

$$= 60x - 40 - 4x + 1.6x^2 - 0.1x^3$$

$$= 56x - 40 + 1.6x^2 - 0.1x^3 \qquad 0 \le x \le 30$$

$$P'(x) = 56 + 3.2x - 0.3x^2$$

$$0 = 56 + 3.2x - 0.3x^2$$

We solve this equation by using the quadratic formula. $a = -0.3$, $b = 3.2, c = 56$.

$$x = \frac{-b \pm \sqrt{b^2 - 4ac}}{2a}$$

$$= \frac{-3.2 \pm \sqrt{3.2^2 - 4(-0.3)(56)}}{-0.6}$$

$$= \frac{-3.2 \pm \sqrt{77.44}}{-0.6}$$

$$= \frac{-3.2 \pm 8.8}{-0.6}$$

$$x = 20 \qquad x = -9.33$$

We reject the negative solution. Since the profit function is continuous on the closed interval [0, 30], we compare the value of $P(x)$ at $x = 20$ with its values at the interval endpoints.

$$P(0) = -40 \qquad P(20) = 920 \qquad P(30) = 380$$

The maximum profit occurs when 20 cameras are sold daily.

10. This is an inventory problem. We let x represent the size of each printing in units of 1000 books. The storage (holding) cost is

$$H(x) = \text{(annual storage cost per item)}\left(\frac{x}{2}\right)$$

$$= 600\left(\frac{x}{2}\right)$$

$$= 300x$$

The ordering cost is

$$O(x) = \text{(cost per printing)(number of printings)}$$

$$= \text{(cost per printing)}\left(\frac{q}{x}\right)$$

$$= (3750)\left(\frac{200}{x}\right)$$

Remember, q is in *thousands*.

$$= 750{,}000x^{-1}$$

The total printing cost, $3 \times 200{,}000 = \$600{,}000$ can be ignored (see note on page 218).

$$C(x) = H(x) + O(x)$$

$$= 300x + 750{,}000x^{-1}$$

$$C'(x) = 300 - 750{,}000x^{-2}$$

$$0 = 300 - \frac{750{,}000}{x^2}$$

$$\frac{750{,}000}{x^2} = 300$$

$$300x^2 = 750{,}000$$

$$x^2 = 2500$$

$$x = 50$$

To minimize cost, each printing should be 50,000 copies.